Value-driven Project Planning

J. ALPHEY

ISBN: 1533059926
ISBN-13: 978-1533059925

Contents

Preface

We read about failing projects every day. Building projects which seem to have gone out of control, IT projects that seem to leave companies in a worse state than they started, change projects which spend money but seem to have no effect. It is easy to see the world of projects as being in crisis. Yet more and more organisations are delivering value through projects because there are strong perceived benefits to this approach.

This means that more people are involved in projects. Some organisations have put in place individuals with a title such as "project manager", "program manager", "scrum master" or similar. Some have no such experts with training and time to focus on these skills. And where these experts exist they will be expected to master project management skills, but this does not mean they are the only people to practice them. Effective working within projects requires an understanding of project skills.

These techniques apply at many levels in a project, from a program(me) manager breaking down a multi-year improvement activity into a set of stages which will be implemented as projects, to a team leader working out the best way to structure the work of a small team to deliver their short term objectives.

The motivation for this book came from my experiences in running project training between 2013 and 2016. I was running around 150 contact hours of training a month, mostly to people who hadn't had the opportunity of formal project training before, although many had extensive project experience. The delegates asked me to focus on the key, practical areas which added the most value and so the "Value-driven" approach was born. The book is intended for anyone who would like to be more effective in their involvement with project planning, whether they see themselves as planners, they give inputs into plans, or they need to use the plans of others.

About this book

Over the years 1999 to 2016 I held a range of Project Director roles at a UK-based semiconductor company which I will call "ChipCo" to keep it anonymous. Over this time, this grew from a small organisation almost entirely in the UK to a thriving and highly profitable FTSE100 multinational with 30 sites. I led the project management team in the core semiconductor design business and then owned and developed the corporate approach to project management.

> *We had a challenging project environment. Design cycles might take 2 to 3 years. The designs were innovative Research and Development, but delivered into customer integration projects with tight and fixed schedules. In the semiconductor industry quality is critical - a customer having to make a design change to fix a defect might cost a million dollars to make a new wafer mask, or much worse if a device were in volume production.*

To address these challenges we developed principles and good practice in project management which helped the company to be hugely successful at project delivery. I worked with great teams across many countries, leading and coaching to project success and learning from every interaction.

This book shares some of my learning and experiences about effective project approaches while in these roles. I make no claim to having invented the concepts. Some are classical project management and date back to the mid-20th century. Some have come from the learnings of other companies, especially with the growth of "agile" concepts. Others evolved from the interactions of many teams as we worked out how to solve problems.

This isn't a book that aims to make you "qualified" in a specific process. It's a book about how real teams learned to deliver world class projects. I hope that it is of value, whatever projects you are running.

This book focusses specifically on planning. It is not the only area of managing projects that matters, but it is a key discipline and one where I have seen good approaches being well practiced. If you want to learn more about the Planning Graveyard, or the Four Horsemen of Project Planning, read on...

Acknowledgements

This book is inspired by my own experiences and would never have existed without the talented teams that I have worked with and the constant learnings that I took away from project interactions. I learned something new about projects and teams constantly. I learned even more when I had the chance to sit in another office halfway across the world and work with a team on what we could share and learn from their latest project. My thanks to all of the teams who welcomed me and shared their thinking. It seems almost unfair to single out individuals or groups, but special thanks to a few people at "ChipCo", with no diminishing of my gratitude to others.

To the Austin team for evenings idea-swapping at the Salt Lick and to the Bangalore team for showing me the power and energy of self-belief, to Tudor for reminding me what is on the card, Ken for being honest, John for often seeing it like I do, Shyam for showing me that there is always good beer if you know where to look and to Steve for getting me writing.. And thanks to Paul, Steve, John and Susan for reviewing the book.

More than anyone, my thanks to Liz, Tristan and Jack for making the journey worthwhile.

> *We are uncovering better ways of developing ...*
> *by doing it and helping others do it*
>
> **The Agile Manifesto**

Examples and principles

Project management is all about practical application. As well as good practice, this book will include some of my own experiences with project planning. We didn't get everything right, but we tried to learn from the mistakes even more than the successes.

 Project experiences are shown in the text like this. These are the "narrative" of the book and discuss what I have personally experienced with the teams with which I've worked. Both the good and the less good.

I have always found that others have put key ideas more elegantly than I could hope to do, and in the tradition of "standing on the shoulders of giants" I hope you will find the quotes thought-provoking.

Quotes are shown in the text like this.

Key principles are shown in the text like this.

 This book is not intended to be a text book full of problems to wade through. However, this symbol marks suggestions for you could try out for yourself, or to just take a break from the book and think about how the subject applies in your own projects. Answers, where appropriate, are at the end of the book.

 I have seen many projects falter or fail due to issues which could be tracked back to planning. Where I cover areas that have proved to be significant risks of project failure, these are marked in the text with "gravestones" as shown to the left here. These build the "Project Graveyard" of project failures.

Chapter 1

What is "Value-driven"?

High value project activities tend to focus on the project at hand and the people involved more than on adherence to standardised rules. There are many specific project methodologies which use standardised language, stages, documents and rules and the consistency brings some benefit to an organisation. These include the Bodies of Knowledge (BoKs) from APM (Association for Project Management) and PMI (Project Management Institute), Prince2 and Scrum to name but a few. It is a bewilderingly large field. Google returns nearly 400,000 hits for "Project Methodology", Wikipedia lists fifteen different international standards without considering the myriad of company-specific approaches.

Value-driven Project Management is about focusing your time on the areas which give the most value to you and to your business. This book is not a specific methodology but includes a set of concepts which should be understood, to some degree, by everyone working in projects. In particular, this book recommends that you focus on the project at hand and the people involved and on team work and communication more than on adherence to standardised rules. These are central tenets of "Agile" approaches and the book will be drawing from ideas viewed as "Agile" as well as those viewed as more traditional project management. Where ideas strongly represent Agile crossover, they are marked with this symbol. Above all, Value-driven project management is pragmatic:

> *Pragmatic: Dealing with things ... in a way that is based on practical rather than theoretical considerations*
>
> *Oxford English Dictionary*

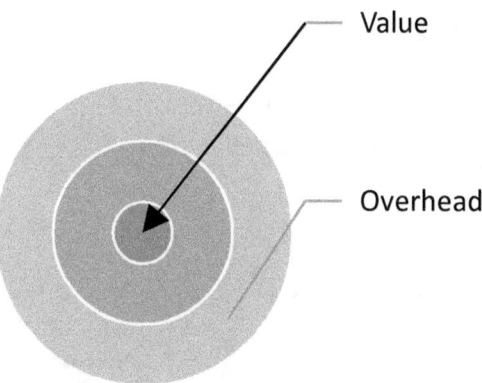

Figure 1- Focus on value

Lines not to be crossed

In every industry there will be lines that cannot be crossed and rules that must not be broken. These are typically about legal compliance and limiting business risk, so that the project cannot put the business as a whole at risk, whether financial or reputational. Every project team needs to know where the boundaries lie. This is partly to reduce risk on the business but also because to truly empower teams they must know the limits of their authority. Without clarity on these rules, the team will constantly be "slapped" for transgressing against unknown rules and will typically respond by losing autonomy and innovation.

> *When I was in an Intellectual Property licensing environment, the control of knowledge was critical. You are licensing designs based on patents. When knowledge is (literally) money, you must be careful to use only what you own or have a legal right to, and to deliver only what you intended to those entitled to receive it. This was central to the project approaches used and how we designed review and release processes. It could be a big cultural shift for new graduates moving from a world where you research, reuse and borrow to one where that is impossible.*

Travelling the same road

These are a set of defined processes and rules in a package, usually under a branded name. These might include "Prince2" and "Scrum" as widely used examples. The benefit of a methodology is to package together a set of processes which are internally consistent. This standardisation gives benefits in terms of training and most importantly in terms of language. The terms used are often not intuitive but if understood by all will allow rapid communication and also a reduced chance of misunderstanding.

When a Prince2 practitioner talks about a "Project Initiation Document" or a "Project Brief", he or she knows what these are for and when and how they are used. They know both that these are required and what they are and so the methodology supplies both process (what needs to be done) and language (how to describe it). A Project Brief is a statement that describes the purpose, cost, time and performance requirements, and constraints for a project. A Project Initiation Documentation is a set of documents that brings together the key information needed to start the project.

Methodologies offer rules which teams are expected to adhere to and which will generally give good results. The downside of methodologies is that you can fall into the trap that following the methodology will inherently manage the project. All methodologies need to be "tailored" to the company or project needs, and the rules applied because they have value in the context. There is a large market in methodology qualifications and training but these do not replace the need for skilled practitioners.

A learning organisation

Good practices are techniques in project management which are proven to be effective in some or all project situations. Every project organisation should put effort into identifying, promoting and training good practices which work for their environment. Value-driven project management is rooted in this approach of identification and sharing of good practice, which could come from a range of project methodologies and should be available to everyone on the project.

Different terms can be used instead of "Good Practice" - the term "Best Practice" is often used. I standardised on "Good Practice" after we concluded that "Best Practice" can imply that you have achieved perfection and have no need for further improvement. "Good Practice" conveys better the key message of continuous improvement. It's "good" but be aware there may always be a "better" out there if you can find it.

Project Management skills are valuable and applicable to everyone working on projects.

Project Managers, if they exist in an organisation, are experts in these skills but everyone on the project will use the skills.

Maintaining your balance

All three of the above – Rules, Methodologies and Good Practice - have their value in how an organisation runs projects. Getting the balance right between these is important as there is value in each. While a methodology could be seen as a flat pack construction set, complete with instructions to put together a quick project, good practices are like a toolkit – they require skill and knowledge to apply but can achieve powerful results.

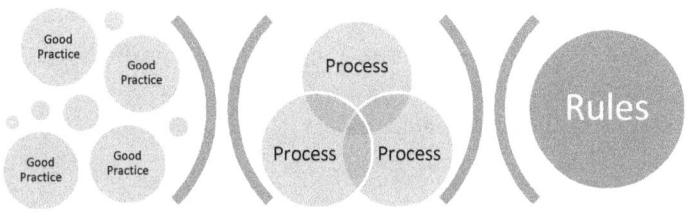

Figure 2 - Project balance

> *I used the terms "Standards" and "Managed Variations" to cover this balancing act. "Standards" were the areas where rules and methodologies were important to the business, avoiding error, building learning and simplifying ramp-up and training. "Variations" were where specific technologies or groups had produced good practices tailored to their own needs. The word "Managed" emphasised how important it is that good practices are maintained to the same quality as the "pre-packaged" methodologies.*

It's easy to get distracted into rules, process and measuring compliance and to forget that these aren't the end goal, which is to deliver value to the business, using projects as a method to achieve this. The value to the business comes from the outputs generated by activities of the team - a set of rules are necessary but don't directly generate value. It is easy to develop processes because you can, not because they are needed. From a value-driven approach we would hope that most of the management time should be spent on the project and the team, not on the process. This is an "80:20" case, where 80% of the value comes from activities specific to the team and the project and only 20% from the framework used.

Planning is one of the functions that support and enable the team and is not just a set of process steps to be performed. The most effective project management matches the insightful quote below.

> *If you want to build a ship, don't drum up the men to gather wood, divide the work and give orders.*
> *Instead, teach them to yearn for the vast and endless sea.*
> *As for the future, your task is not to foresee it, but to enable it*
>
> *Antoine de Saint-Exupery*

Project Management should involve at most 20% of time following methodology rules and at least 80% work specific to the project, its team and stakeholders.

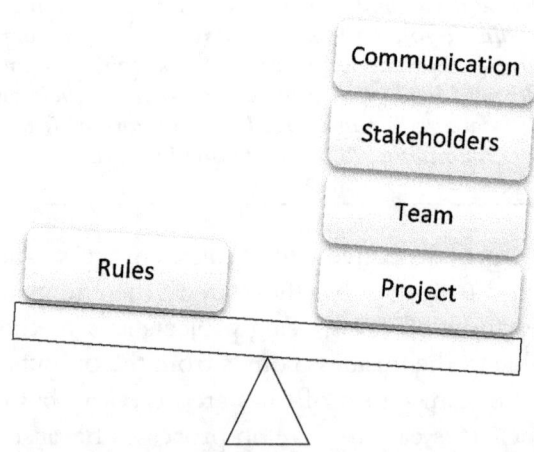

Figure 3- Getting the balance right

Chapter 2

What is Planning?

Chapter 2 Exercise – Why Plan?

If you are reading this book, you are interested in planning. Take a minute or two to think about what planning really is. Talk to one or two of your friends and colleagues. After all, this is only Chapter 2 and we have a whole book ahead of us to discuss planning methods, approaches and good practice. Let's decide why you thought it important enough to buy the book and what you would like to gain from it.

So to start things off, what do you think a plan is for? Take a bit of time to think about why you **want** to be better at planning. You're investing time in a plan, so what do you expect to get back in return? We will be looking at answers to this in the next chapter.

The four horsemen of project planning

This book is designed to present a structured approach to planning which can be applied to a wide range of projects. But projects are all different and techniques will vary. Ralph Stacey argued that business environments can be characterised by two parameters as shown below (Stacey RD, "Strategic management and organisational dynamics: the challenge of complexity", 2002)

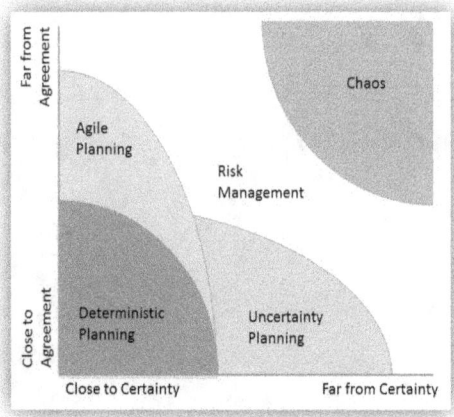

Figure 4 - Planning styles and the Stacey Matrix (from Stacey 2002)

Degree of certainty. - This relates to the quality of information available for decision making. Good quality information leads to rational, analytical planning.

Degree of agreement. - This relates to how much the involved people agree with the approach to be taken as a result of the information available. A high degree of agreement leads to low level of change.

As the environments tend towards increasing complexity the project manager must look beyond the simple predictive planning approaches. Increasingly these more uncertain environments are the ones in which teams find themselves. The Stacey Matrix leads to the four key sets of project management tools for dealing with different environments. We can consider these as "***The four horsemen of project planning***":

Figure 5 – The "Four Horsemen of Project Planning"

This book focuses on the first two environments below.

First there is the environment where there is a high degree of both certainty and agreement. This does not mean problems are trivial. Far from it, they can be complicated, involving large amounts of work, but it is known, or at least knowable. This environment is **Deterministic Planning**.

If we reduce the degree of certainty, we move along the horizontal axis in Stacey's diagram. Although we still agree what we want to do, we find that it is harder to predict what will happen as a result. Estimates are more uncertain, unexpected tasks may occur, higher defect rates and rework may be expected. The tools to look at this environment are addressed in the section on **Managing Uncertainty**.

A future book will address a Value-driven approach to more complex environments .

> *Outcomes emerge in the interplay of everyone's plans and intentions and no one can control the interplay.*
>
> *Ralph D. Stacey, Complexity and Organizational Reality*

The other dimension in Stacey's diagram is the degree of agreement. As this decreases, the environment becomes fast changing as priorities shift, market needs change and customers clamour for attention. The doubt here may be all about value – deciding what would be the best decision for the business. This is the environment which is addressed by **Agile Planning**.

As both certainty and agreement reduce, the project environment becomes more complex with more interactions and less ability to see cause and effect. In this domain, a critical factor becomes the ability of the project team in **Managing Risk**.

Deterministic Planning

The basic "bread and butter" of project planning is the ability to take a problem and to build a plan to address that problem. This is covered in the first chapters of this book, which introduce the basic concepts of planning and outline an approach that can be taken to building a plan from an initial project concept through defining the project, planning the scope and activities to be completed and then building a project schedule. There are a series of techniques involved in this with which everyone involved in projects should be familiar.

This approach to projects is based on projects which are highly predictive. This means that a plan can be built and then delivery will follow the plan with a reasonable level of accuracy. It is an approach to planning which has been developed since the formalisation of projects in the 1950s and summarised as "deterministic planning". Perhaps few projects are truly that predictive, especially in today's business environment, but the tools and approaches used are a starting point for planning approaches.

> *Determinism: all events... are ultimately determined by causes ... external to the will*
>
> ***Oxford English Dictionary***

Deterministic planning is based on decomposing (breaking down) a problem. These are split into a smaller set of problems which are then planned and sequenced. In more recent years some writers and some project approaches have questioned whether projects are fundamentally predictive enough to use this approach, or at least wholly to use this approach. The techniques involved are valuable as good practices, but remember they will need to be appropriately applied and tailored for the project being managed.

Figure 6 -Deterministic planning

Deterministic planning skills are fundamental and all practitioners should be familiar with them, though many projects may need to introduce more techniques.

Managing Uncertainty

Deterministic planning looks as though we are trying to predict the future. Planners cannot do this, however hard they try. As uncertainty increases we see that a plan is a model, chosen from many alternative plans. It is used as a tool to set direction and manage decisions, through prioritisation, tracking or reporting.

Uncertainty is not a subject which is widely discussed and understood. There are challenges in how we manage high levels of uncertainty in an effective way. This requires the tools for addressing uncertainty, for modelling and communicating it and for ensuring that an uncertain project has a high level of likelihood of successful delivery.

Uncertainty Management takes the reader beyond the basic tools of project management into a better understanding of how to apply these in a more uncertain environment.

Risk Management

Risk Management is central to project methodologies. The project team must anticipate and manage threats which could impact the project. Risk is kept distinct here from Uncertainty as it relates to specific, macro events with cause and effect which can be directly managed. Many authors blur the two but the methods for managing them tend to be distinct.

Risk Management is, or should be, central to good project planning. Indeed there is an argument that Risk is the key driver and that planning itself is a Risk Management strategy. But effective Risk Management is not a trivial task. Many teams struggle to anticipate and manage areas of Risk. This becomes more critical as the project environment becomes more changeable. Value-driven approaches to Risk Management will be in a follow-on volume.

Agile Planning

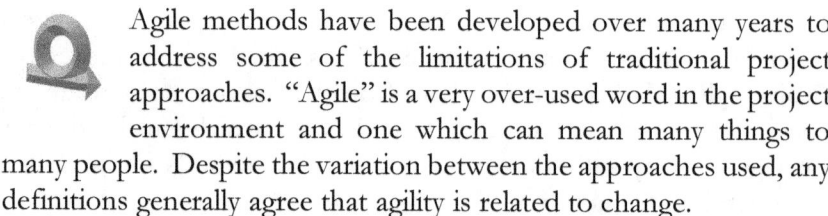Agile methods have been developed over many years to address some of the limitations of traditional project approaches. "Agile" is a very over-used word in the project environment and one which can mean many things to many people. Despite the variation between the approaches used, any definitions generally agree that agility is related to change.

> *Agile: able to move quickly and easily*
>
> ***Oxford English Dictionary***

All projects need to have agility, but as the level of agreement reduces, the likelihood of change increases. Modern business environments often need something more than the classical contract-and-change approach where every re-prioritisation results in replan, expense and delay. The Agile movement has been revolutionising ideas of how to run projects in this sort of environment and agile planning looks at how planning is used in an Agile project, where change is embraced as a chance of optimisation, not rejected as an inconvenience. Value-driven approaches to Agile Planning will be in a follow-on volume.

Chapter 3

The challenge of planning

Why do we plan?

There is considerable work involved in building a plan, so we need to be clear on the benefits in return. Value-driven project management, after all, is about maximising the value from the project management work, so we need to be very sure why we are making a plan. A plan is not a crystal ball and does not let us see the future. Nor does it deliver any of the work involved in the project. The plan is a model which lets us shape that future by giving us some powerful tools and framework for making decision.

The value of the plan comes from what you have learned through the planning. This is typically more important than the detail of the planning document itself. Many military leaders have made comments to that effect. You don't win a battle by comparing your fixed plan with your opponent's.

> *Plans are nothing, planning is everything*
>
> *Dwight D. Eisenhower*

A plan allows us to make decisions in advance. By predicting events that will occur in the future, we can anticipate and control them. This is the alternative to "crisis management" where a project is driven by problems and issues and the team is in a constant reaction mode.

A plan also allows us to prioritise actions. By seeing cause and effect we can decide to move tasks earlier, increase the focus on specific activities or take certain decisions now with a clearer understanding of the consequences on the project.

A plan allows us to set expectations. We can be clear about what we are able to deliver. We can set realistic expectations and on the project's completion we can demonstrate that we have delivered on them.

A plan allows us to communicate what we need to achieve success. This removes doubt about what our suppliers need to give (teams, goods or money) in order for the project to succeed, and allows the suppliers to arrange their own plans to match

Finally a plan gives us a model to compare with real events. This will give us warning of variance between the actual events and the expected events and some understanding of what the consequences of the variance may be.

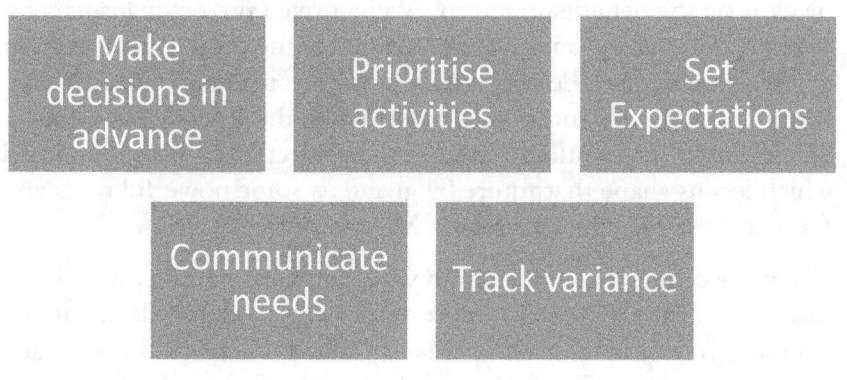

Figure 7 – Purpose of a plan

So why don't we plan?

> *The nicest thing about not planning is that failure comes*
> *as a complete surprise rather than being preceded*
> *by a period of worry and depression.*
>
> **Sir John Harvey Jones**

If plans have value, why is it that we so often see projects that don't plan? There is a strong temptation, perhaps inherent in human nature, to avoid planning and instead to leap into action. Why do we see this so often? There are many barriers to planning. Some are real, some imagined, and some apply differently across project teams and cultures. Below are what seem to be some of the top problems in starting to build a plan.

- A conscious belief that there is no time to plan and we have to start on the work. Here the view is that planning time reduces development time. This is especially prevalent when there clearly isn't enough time available.
- A feeling that planning will expose all of the difficulties in the project and reveal that it will fail. As in Sir John's quote, planning is seen as the tool that takes away the hope of possible success.
- A fear that documenting the approach to be taken will make it visible and challenged. Perhaps the approach will not be allowed and a different plan will be imposed. By "hiding" the plan any review is avoided and so the team can progress as desired.
- An inability or lack of desire to start on the plan because of lack of planning skills. Many projects are very complicated and starting to create a plan is a daunting task. So daunting in some cases that the plan is never started.
- A fear that planning prevents flexibility and innovation and that by building a plan you may be preventing the best solution from being adopted.

> *I have experienced all of the above issues hindering the creation of a plan. Projects were always tight on time and the temptation to "just get started" was huge, but after a while people realised this was counterproductive and took longer in the end. The concern that planning will expose issues is more insidious. In some groups raising concerns could be seen as negative, or as "not being a team player". This and the "flying under the radar" approach to avoid review are about the culture of the team and it took time to achieve the right level of belief in planning.*

Planning and conflict

One key feature of planning is that it always causes conflict. This seems to be inherent in the nature of planning. A sponsor wants an outcome from a project and has built a picture in his/her head of what this outcome will be and how much it will cost to obtain it. Project management is very much "the art of the possible" so the planning activity has to take this desire into the realms of possibility, considering all of the constraints on a real project. In doing this, it will typically restrict the outcomes to what is realistic, and assess costs and requirements in a more detailed and complete way. This will generally lead to a proposed plan which is less attractive than the original concept.

> *It is an interesting question why an initial proposal is generally more attractive than a fully planned project. We would see this on every project. The original concept would come from marketing, who were focussed on what would be attractive to customers, and from the more inventive technologists, who tended to be optimists. Of course, this isn't a bad thing but you must get the planning involved early enough to avoid over-committing.*

The sponsor will inevitably be disappointed as they wanted to have more value for less cost. How a planner responds to this is critical to the success of the planning process. A natural reaction for many is to defer the conflict by agreeing a plan that is attractive to the sponsor, especially when the sponsor is vocal and senior. This behaviour is often rewarded in organisations but risks locking the team into an impossible plan resulting in a failed delivery. The conflict will always occur and the only choice is whether it occurs at the planning stage or (more disastrously) at the delivery stage.

This is a key message for teams to understand and it was something that I focussed on for both training and coaching. The choice is being shouted at early (for an unattractive plan) or being shouted at later (for failing to deliver). There is no planning option where you don't get shouted at.

Conflict is inevitable in planning as sponsors want more for less. This must be accepted in planning rather than deferred to delivery.

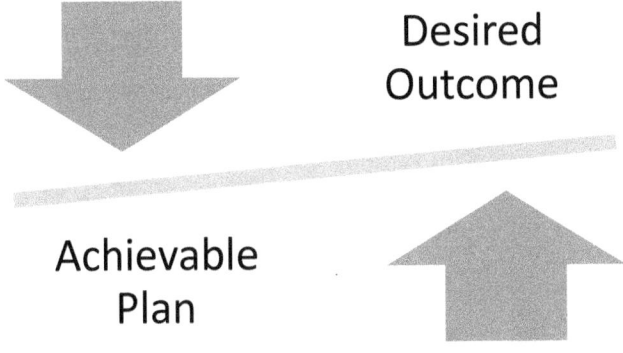

Figure 8 - Conflict in planning

You cannot see the future

Planning, however well performed, cannot truly predict the future. One seductive delusion in deterministic planning is that once the planning has been done, you truly know what will happen on the project. This belief that the plan is perfect has been criticised for leading to the "command and control" approach to project management which is not only demoralising but also ineffective for any but the most simple projects. However there is a persistent, perhaps cultural, belief that it is only the planner's skill that prevents perfect prediction. This belief in the ability of "perfect analysis" can be seen in cultural themes such as Conan Doyle's "Sherlock Holmes".

> Sherlock Holmes's quick eye took in my occupation, and he shook his head with a smile as he noticed my questioning glances. "Beyond the obvious facts that he has at some time done manual labour, that he takes snuff, that he is a Freemason, that he has been in China, and that he has done a considerable amount of writing lately, I can deduce nothing else."
>
> **The Red-Headed League, Sir Arthur Conan Doyle**

In a "Value-driven" approach, over-planning is as dangerous as under-planning. You need to keep a sense of realism about how accurately you can plan. Don't waste time endlessly chasing more "accuracy" when you know that it will not help you define or control the project.

Planning and culture

The key issues that lead to resistance to planning all have their roots in organisational culture. For a business to succeed it must of course have a strategy. But a strategy alone is no more than a nice set of slides unless it can be delivered. To have an **achievable** strategy, there needs to be a link from strategy through to delivery. Unfortunately it is easy for each layer of the organisation to add its own mindset, overpromising to gain favours or resource, wild optimism for "pet projects", overestimation where other work is desired. So a promising strategy may be far separated from the reality of what the company can and will deliver.

> *Culture eats strategy for breakfast*
>
> *Peter Drucker*

 To be effective, project management needs support from the organisation. If the organisation imposes unrealistic schedules, lacks trust in its teams, fails to support its teams with coaching and review, or fails to have open and honest dialogue about plans, it will be limited in what it can achieve. Worse still, if it actively penalises project teams for honest planning, it can get locked into a cycle of fictional plans followed by delivery failure, without ever realising where the problem lies.

> *Drive out fear*
>
> *From Deming's 14 points for total quality management*

While I have been fortunate that the environment where I worked was generally very open and focussed on achievable projects, I have also seen teams where this is not the case. Team culture has been central to successful implementation of planning improvement. I recall one team that was adamant that a planning approach wasn't necessary. They limped through a number of projects until eventually they hit one that was just too complex and were badly burned. To their credit however, they realised that the approach to planning had been a fundamental limitation to their success and the group culture turned around. Cultural change will take time. Sometimes teams will need to learn from their own experiences (although learning from others is often cheaper). But Deming's message is a key one – "drive out fear". Teams are only enabled to learn and improve if the organisation is more focussed on learning than blame.

It is critical that teams are enabled to achieve success. This requires them to make commitments and deliver on them. To do this, the organisation must build a planning culture. This is far less trivial than it sounds, because many organisations don't start by thinking this way, and cultural change is tough. When an organisation is small, it runs in "startup mode", which is characterised by getting things done, responding to customers and managing crises. An organisation which supports project management needs to evolve away from crisis management into crisis prevention. This can be quite a difficult step for the "startup mode" managers who may have been promoted based on their ability to managed crises (and may actually like the excitement of crises).

I use the phrase "Make projects boring" to highlight the objective here. Great planning takes away some of the crises and makes delivery more predictable. It's unlikely ever to truly become "boring" – there's just too much to do in delivering a project – but it is useful to bring the issue out into the open.

The planning process must be "honest" so that the organisation and the planners genuinely wish to see teams achieve success.

Groupthink in planning

Groupthink is such an important topic it deserves discussion all to itself. Groupthink causes teams to head like lemmings over a cliff that no-one sees coming. It is the tendency of individuals in a group to go along with the team viewpoint because it's hard to speak up against a widely-held opinion.

> *The more amiability and esprit de corps there is among the members of a policy-making in-group, the greater the danger that independent critical thinking will be replaced by groupthink.*
>
> **Irving Janis, US psychologist**

Groupthink is a problem to you when managing a project. On the one hand, you want to build team spirit. You want your team to work together – all of the management teachings are clear you should aim for this. On the other hand, as a planner you want the "independent critical thinking" that Janis says will be affected if you achieve that goal. So how serious a problem is this? Should you really be worried?

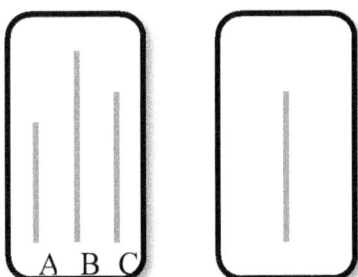

Let's look at an example known as the Asch conformity experiments. This was a series of psychology experiments. You put eight people in a room and you show them two cards. One has three lines on and one has one line. Which line on the first card is the same length as the line on the second card?

Figure 9 – Asch conformity cards

Seems easy? Well, this is a psychology experiment and the "trick" is that seven of the people in the room are secretly part of the experiment. What if they all say the **wrong** answer? A, maybe. What do you do now as the eighth person? As far as you know all seven have genuinely answered "A". Do you stick with "C", which looks correct, or go with "A" to match the others? In these studies in 30% of cases the eighth person went along with the majority. They convinced themselves they had misunderstood, or misread, or something to avoid challenging the majority.

This has huge impacts in planning. Think about Groupthink as we look at planning techniques. How can we make sure we include all of the knowledge from your team if there is such pressure to conform to the "agreed" answer?

One Groupthink situation I tended to experience was when planning with engineering leads. These were the experts and their opinions were highly respected. If the lead walked in to the room, they were expected to come out with "the answer". It wasn't a deliberate action by the lead (or the team), but it's best to leave the expert outside for some discussions.

Planning is an inclusive process. Groupthink is an enemy. Find a way to include everyone's knowledge.

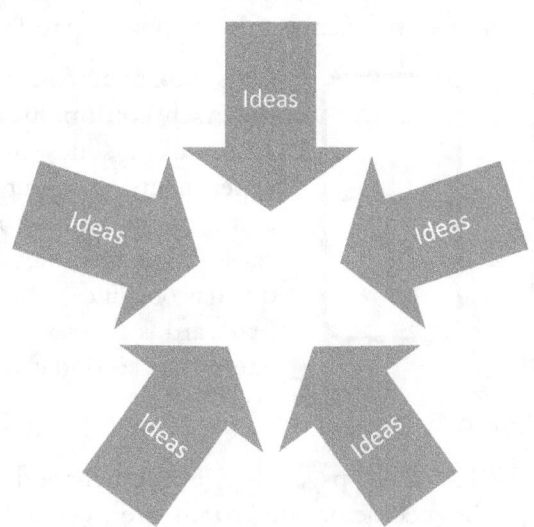

Figure 10 - Planning is an inclusive process

Chapter 4

Defining the Project

Where do we start?

Different people have different ideas of what a "plan" is. Many teams try to start from thinking about tasks, or even about schedule. One reason is that a "plan" is often represented by a Gantt chart. With the growth of project management software that produce Gantt Charts these have become almost the badge of project managers, but remember they are a tool, and like all tools you should be using them as and where they add value.

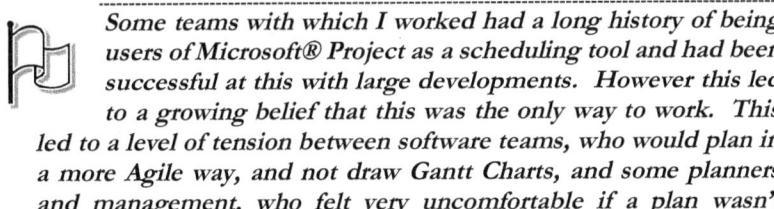 *Some teams with which I worked had a long history of being users of Microsoft® Project as a scheduling tool and had been successful at this with large developments. However this led to a growing belief that this was the only way to work. This led to a level of tension between software teams, who would plan in a more Agile way, and not draw Gantt Charts, and some planners and management, who felt very uncomfortable if a plan wasn't represented in that form.*

A plan comes from a team and isn't generated by an individual. Project management skills are about shaping and facilitating planning. This means as a planner you need to think how to include your team in the planning process, and as we have seen earlier that includes thinking about building a planning culture and avoiding Groupthink in how you work.

Before you can consider the tasks in the project and who will do them (the "how" of delivering) you need to think about the "what". You need to thoroughly understand the context of the project – what you are asked to do and why it is needed. This is the "definition" part of the project and is sometimes rushed – everyone wants to get on with the activities because action suggests progress. But planning is like a pyramid – the definition is at the base and needs to be solid enough to support the rest of the plan. How you capture the definition data will depend on your project approach. The PMI, for example, talk about a "Project Management Plan" which covers all aspects of how the project is set up, organised and run.

It is important to decide, agree and collect this definition of how you will work to manage the project. We used the term "Project Definition" (and this could be a physical document or an online resource). Ensure that the initial definition has been done and then that this is maintained as and if there are any changes.

Case Study – a communication failure

The Mars Climate Orbiter

The Mars Climate Orbiter was a 338 kilogram robotic space probe launched by NASA on December 11, 1998. It was intended to study the Martian climate, atmosphere and surface changes and to act as the communications relay in the Mars Surveyor 1998 program. As such it was a critical piece of the NASA Mars program.

Developing technology for space is a long and complex process and quality is critical. Errors typically cannot be corrected after launch and so every effort is made to get things right. In many ways this is like the environment I was used to in silicon development. There was a huge investment in this project. $193 million was invested in spacecraft development, $92 million for launch and $43 million for operations.

What happened?

On September 23, 1999, communication with the spacecraft was lost as the spacecraft went into orbital insertion. No contact was regained and the craft crashed into the planet. The only data returned were a few low quality pictures of the planet Mars. Value returned from the investment was effectively zero.

Why did this happen?

This was a major failure and unexpected given the rigorous processes in place in NASA. The Mars Climate Orbiter Mishap Investigation looked at where the errors had occurred. Perhaps one team had made a mistake and introduced a defect in hardware or software. Surely this was a failure in the processes used by one of the teams to develop or test functionality. Their conclusion was as follows:

> *The root cause for the loss of the spacecraft was the failure*
> *to use metric units in the coding of a ground software file.*
> *Specifically, thruster performance data in Imperial units*
> *instead of metric was used in the software application code.*
>
> **Mars Climate Orbiter Mishap Investigation Phase I Report**

So what had happened? The software was being developed by two teams, one in the US and one in Europe. One team developed the navigation code and one team the thruster control code. Both teams wrote code that functioned exactly as intended. The failure was in how the two pieces of code worked together. Software that calculated the total impulse produced by thruster firings calculated results in pound-seconds (US Imperial units). The trajectory calculation software then used these results to update the predicted position of the spacecraft, believing them to be in newton-seconds (metric units). As a result the wrong amount of rocket thrust was generated, firing the craft into the planet.

What can we learn?

Many textbooks refer to project management in terms of delivery to time, cost and scope. They describe the role of project management as primarily to achieve all of these. A blind following of this rule can be dangerous. We must always ensure that the project is set up correctly with the right objectives. The business has created the project for a purpose and the project must deliver the intended value. The Mars Climate Orbiter failed not because the teams failed to deliver what they were asked, but because what they were asked for did not deliver the intended outcome.

Before planning begins we need to look at the context within which the project operates. This is the purpose of the definition stage of the project. This builds the foundations for the project. Like any foundations, lack of attention leads to a risk of failure however good subsequent planning and execution may be.

The Mars Climate Orbiter example seems extreme, but I recall a project "lessons learned" session with a software team. There had been a major customer incident with a new software release. It had required an update to a customer's server which the customer was unable to make. This was "not a bug" because everything worked to specification. The team had a narrow definition of "bug" which was about functional failure against specification. As a result they were unsure how to proceed when they had a customer issue that was here linked to a requirements problem.

It all starts with success

So where do we start in the planning process? Building a plan can be daunting, especially when the project is producing something new, often starting with very little, and controlling many people over a long timescale. We need to start with a vision – something to head for. Call this "Success". The starting point for any project is to understand what is Success. If you truly understand success you can learn what you need to make or deliver to achieve that success. You also have a measurement scale which lets you set priorities and make decisions. Defining Success also gives you an understanding of when to stop. It may sound obvious, but when you have planned, and later executed, everything needed for success, then you have succeeded. Understanding success is also critical to your team. The project may be tough and everyone may have to work very hard, but the team must feel in control of their destiny and must understand on what basis they will be judged.

I worked with very skilled project teams, but on many occasions they found themselves on projects where success was not clearly defined at the start. I remember one example with a major microprocessor development. The team had been given a target performance figure which was seen as challenging. And they took it as a challenge. They worked long hours, they came up with imaginative solutions and eventually they not only reached the target but came back to the marketing team to proudly announce they had exceeded the target by 20%. There was a long pause and then one of the marketing team said "so if this product is 20% faster than we asked for, what do we sell next year?" Success had been to hit a performance target, not to exceed it.

Success means people

> *Organisation doesn't really accomplish anything.*
> *Plans don't accomplish anything, either.*
> *Theories of management don't much matter.*
> *Endeavors succeed or fail because of the people involved.*
>
> **Colin Powell, US Secretary of State**

Most people would agree that projects are about people and not about process and paperwork. But many project teams forget this in this critical planning stage. The desire to rush to getting tasks on paper makes people forget, or side-step, the awkward fact that the success that we want to understand is not an absolute. Success is subjective and a function of the people involved. So any plan that does not focus on the people is never going to succeed fully. Success for the project and for the team will be judged by the stakeholders. What may in your mind be a shining clear success - "we delivered on time" - risks being a shifting mass of perceptions and interpretations. So your plan needs a grounding in this area, and this is the key topic of stakeholders.

This is a chance to think about your stakeholders and about building a plan for how you are going to manage them. This is part of your plan just as much as those tasks.

> *Stakeholder: A person with an interest or concern*
>
> **Oxford English Dictionary**

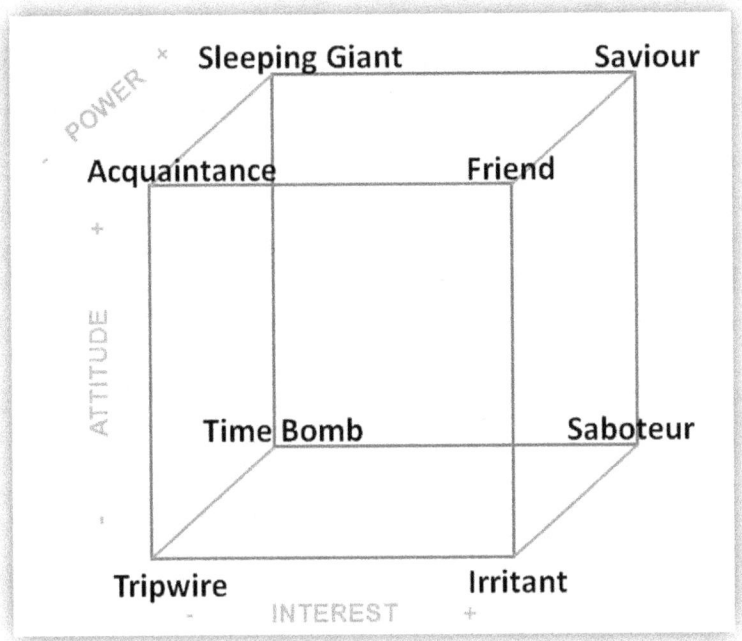

Figure 11 - Stakeholder analysis (after Lucidus model)

There are many models for assessing stakeholders – this one from Lucidus Consulting (in Lucid Thought 24). They propose three dimensions of measurement:

- Power - Does the stakeholder have power over your project?
- Interest - How interested is he or she in what you are doing?
- Attitude - Do they agree with the project?

I've found this to be very effective in discussing stakeholders with teams, if a little harder to draw than a two-dimensional model. The model also includes great names for the extremes as below. So for example a "Time Bomb" is someone who has power over your project (perhaps he or she is supplying something you need or approving a project activity), has a negative attitude, so they don't like what you are doing, but has little interest so is unlikely to take action. However, he or she could be a real risk to the project if they do.

Chapter 4 Exercise - Stakeholders

Time spent analysing stakeholders and planning approaches for them is usually time well spent. This is an area for teams to practice. Think this through on your project and try out some examples now. What would you do with the following stakeholders on your project? Maybe you have real examples from a project you are currently running and can consider what you might plan for managing those individuals..

- A Sleeping Giant – he or she has a positive attitude, a high level of power over the project and a low level of interest.
- A Saboteur, who has a negative attitude, high power and low interest?

Plan out some strategies to manage these – suggestions are at the end of the book.

Setting off on the right path

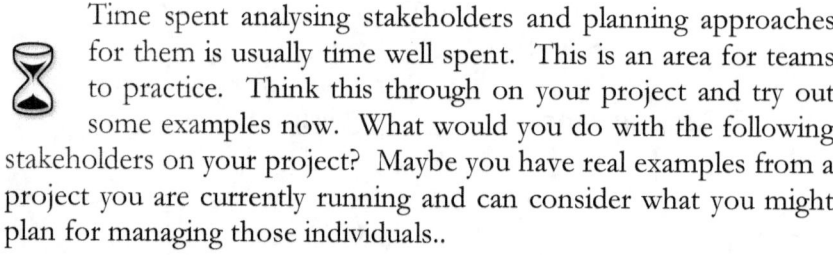

Requirements are one of the key parts of defining the project. Set out on the wrong path and however good your plan you will never achieve project success. So it's worth focussing some time on the key points around Requirements. Firstly, we need to be clear what we mean by a Requirement.

> Requirement: A thing that is needed or wanted
>
> **Oxford English Dictionary**

Requirements are clearly closely linked to success. They represent what the stakeholders need (or want) from the project in order for them to rate the project as a success. And in order to achieve project success you need to make sure that all stakeholders have an opportunity to input into, or to review, the requirements. This is clearly going to be a significant endeavour. We want to capture requirements from all of the stakeholders. We also want to make sure we capture them in a way that is clear that we have delivered what was asked for. This will allow us to define and then deliver project success.

In the approach that I was using, completing the Requirements capture was a key part of moving from the definition to the planning stage of the project. And it is important that pragmatism comes into play. You want the Requirements agreed, but you can't stall the planning waiting for the very last detail. This was the sort of judgement call that distinguished the really good project teams.

What does a Requirement look like? Ideally we will be capturing **who** needs or wants an outcome, and **what** is needed. It is important to understand the problem that needs to be solved and where the **value** is to the user. This is sometimes described using the idea of a "story" – the user wants to act in a particular way and the "user story" describes what he or she wants to do. Importantly a Requirement is not a design or a solution, it is a statement that a problem must be solved. The "story" idea can help here. When Requirements specify how something is done, rather than what needs to be done, they start to constrain the project team to a solution which may not be optimal. Remember that Requirements should not be specifying the solution but the need.

The last part of the Requirement is how it will be verified. Since Requirements are tightly linked to success, it is critical that each Requirement can be demonstrated so that project success is clearly agreed. Linked to the verification, any Requirement must be clear and unambiguous, which typically means it should be stated in simple, quite formal language.

All Requirements are not equal. It is important to have some scoring for importance of Requirements. We will gain some idea of the cost and schedule for delivering everything ("the gold solution") and we may find that this is too expensive or too late for the market. It is rare indeed that a plan can deliver everything that was originally desired. There are several scoring systems used, but where all Requirements are gathered and planned at the beginning, a good approach is known as "MoSCoW".

This rates Requirements into four categories:

- "Must Have" – these form your success criteria for the project.
- "Should Have" – these are important and would be expected to be included, but in the worst case can be abandoned
- "Could Have" – these are useful and will be included in the planning but can be dropped in the planning or execution if necessary to hit the dates.
- "Won't Have" – although these have value, it is agreed that these will not be included.

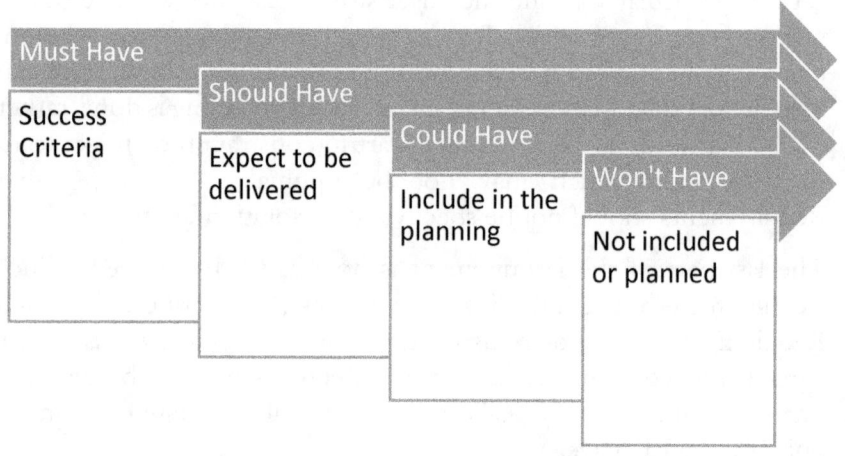

Figure 12 - MoSCoW prioritisation

There's a significant challenge in getting a set of Requirements agreed. This is increased when prioritisation needs to be included as well. Every Requirement was proposed by someone, and to that individual they are usually important, possibly critical. Try to de-personalise the discussions and focus on customer value from the overall package, rather than have everyone defend their own Requirements. However, accept this is another area of conflict and unless well managed you risk ending up with an unachievable list of "Must Have" items and nothing in the other categories.

Chapter 4 Exercise - Requirements

This comes from an "Advertisement and Specification for a Heavier-Than-Air Flying Machine", U.S. Army Signal Corps 1907.

Sufficiently simple in its construction and operation to permit an intelligent man to become proficient in its use within a reasonable length of time

Is this a good Requirement which you would allow on your project?

Think about what you would create if you were given this as the Requirement.

Chapter 5

Deterministic Planning

Why the basics matter

Deterministic planning is the process of building a plan for a project where the environment is stable. This is a key set of steps and skills for anyone working on projects to master. The toolkit for deterministic planning can be applied to most projects. When the project has low certainty or low agreement you need to modify or typically extend the approach but you also need to have mastered the basic approaches first.

Case Study – building an icon

The Sydney Opera House

The competition to design the Sydney Opera House was held in January 1957 and was won by the Danish architect Jorn Utzon. However, his original exterior design was so imaginative that it proved structurally impossible to build. He continued working on the designs for another four years of research before the designs were complete.

However, the Australian government, eager to see progress, insisted that construction began straight away with the incomplete design. Not only the exterior was changing - the original design called for two theatres and the government altered this to four theatres during construction.

What happened?

The design complexity, materials requirements and changes involved led to an exceptional level of project overrun. The original estimate for the Sydney Opera House was US$7 million and the final cost was US$102 million, more than 14 times the original estimate. The original planned completion date set by the government was 26 January 1963, which allowed four years to complete the work. It was eventually completed in 1973 after 14 years.

Utzon resigned in February 1966 and when he died in 2008 he had never seen the completed building.

Why did this happen?

Clearly a major factor here was the complex and incomplete nature of the design. The precise shape of the iconic roof curves was not defined and how these would be manufactured had not been addressed. There were at least a dozen different shell designs attempted before one was found which worked.

What made this such an issue was the lack of separation between an investigative, planning stage and the construction stage. Construction began without a clear plan through the fallacy of wanting to show progress. This meant that dates and budgets were committed without plans, and that significant money had to be spent on changes of direction and rework. Indeed some substantial changes were needed, not least a rebuilding of the podium columns which were not strong enough to support the final, redesigned roof.

What can we learn?

The Opera House is an iconic building and cannot be considered a "failure" in any conventional way. However the project to develop it was flawed. Few projects would consider such a level of overrun to be a success. The root cause lies in the early start on construction and the lack of a clear plan and design.

That is not to say that a project must necessarily specify everything in great detail before implementation. As we will see in the companion book, the Agile movement introduced new ways of planning for high-change environments. However, the degree to which activities interrelate, the optimum sequence and the associated risks must be considered before commitments are made. Metaphorically, you should never build your podium without understanding the roof it will hold up.

Knowing what to make

At this point in the planning process you have defined the problem which you need to address. In particular you understand what you need to do to achieve project success. You have a clearly agreed set of requirements for the project and you understand the stakeholders involved and their needs and views for success.

> *Be careful not to rush ahead into planning without the definition of the project being in place. In the process I was using, this was the point for a "gate" at which there was review, discussion and approval of the project definition before proceeding with the planning. This may sound an obvious step, but there is a constant temptation to rush on with the project, even if people aren't quite sure what the project objectives are.*

Product Breakdown

The requirements which have been generated when defining the project are typically at quite a high level. They will represent the needs of the business, of stakeholders and customers. They may be in the form of a measurable goal (achieving a specific performance or a level of improvement in a change project), a piece of functionality or a capability. Sometimes the concept of "Stories" is used, where a story is an outcome told from the viewpoint of the user, not the developer, focussing on the value to that user. These cannot typically be used directly by the project team without a level of further expansion. We need to get from the desired outcomes to the required outputs – what we need to make. The tool for this is a Product Breakdown Structure or PBS. Don't be concerned about the word "Product" here – it's an applicable technique for all types of output, even if you feel your project isn't generating a product.

You'll often see this referred to as a "Work Breakdown Structure" or WBS. However there is a subtle difference. At this point we're not yet thinking about the work to be done, but about the results – the items to be produced. So you need to be focussed on outputs.

What is a Product Breakdown Structure? What we are doing is taking the high level Requirement which we have been given, and breaking it down further and further until we really understand everything that we need to create in order to satisfy the requirement.

> *I've had many reviews with late running projects, and I often found that an immediate response for why the project is late is "poor estimation". However, investigation rarely backed this up. All the evidence was that teams that I worked with weren't too bad at estimating the amount of work to complete a task. The overruns were more often down to tasks that were missed. Building the PBS is the opportunity to ensure that you have considered everything that needs to be done.*

A PBS is a hierarchical breakdown. You take each Requirement and break it down into smaller elements. And then if needed break these down further. At each level you need to make sure you include everything so nothing is missed from your plan.

> Tools advice
> Good tools for hierarchical breakdown are those developed for
> Mind Mapping ™. There are a range on the market, some free to
> download.

Let's look at an example. Imagine that you have been asked to organise a meeting. Let's take this as my top-level requirement:

Figure 13 – PBS of a meeting (level 1)

To plan the meeting you need to think about what exactly you will need to produce. How are you going to subdivide this? You conclude that the important deliverables are the participants, an agreed agenda for the meeting and a room to hold it. So you divide up the problem into those categories as below.

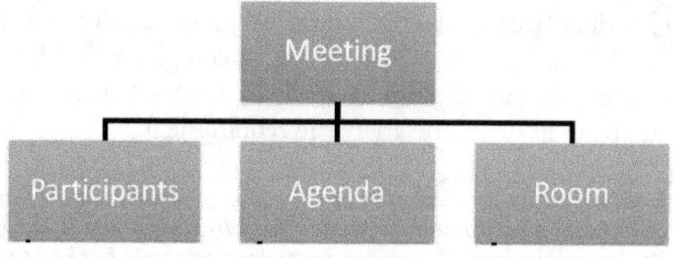

Figure 14 – PBS of a meeting (level 2)

Is this enough? Well, these aren't quite outputs yet, so you will look at one more level of subdivision. For the participants you need defined roles, invitations and confirmation of attendance. For the agenda, you need a defined agenda and also need this to be a circulated document. And finally for the room, you need to have a room chosen and also to ensure that it is a booked and available room.

This gives the next level of your hierarchy as below.

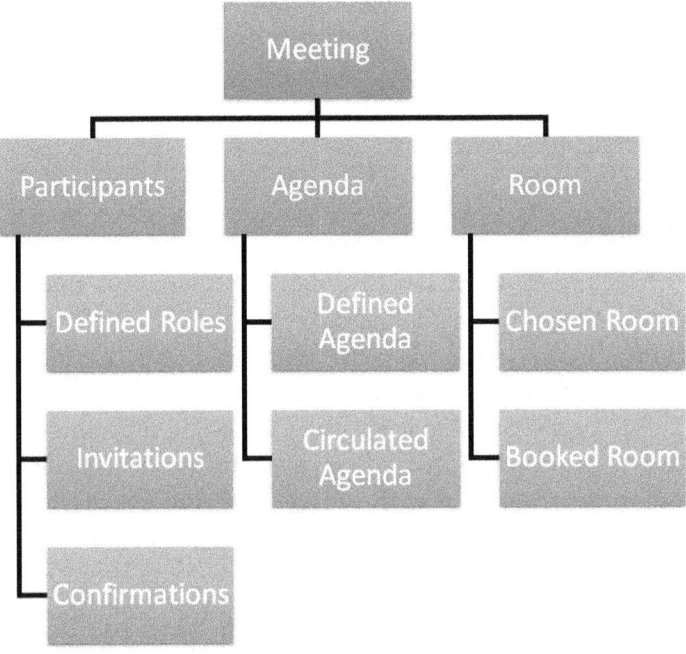

Figure 15 – PBS of a meeting (level 3)

We can see that with the bottom level of the PBS we have come down to a level of clear outputs which we could plan to deliver. So we have taken a large problem and decomposed it into smaller, plannable problems. The top level is often called a "Product" or "Marketing" requirement and represents value to the business, while the bottom level is a "Sub" or "Team" requirement and represents a project output.

It is important to try and make the list of bottom level items as complete as possible. Anything missed here will not become a planned output for the project and so potentially could be a late headache when you realise it is needed. However, there is no "correct" answer for the structure of the PBS - the "mid-levels" do not represent product outputs and a different team might use a different structure to reach the breakdown.

Since the PBS represents outputs, and not work, you should try and use nouns and not verbs throughout. So we have said "Invitations" (the output or result) and not "Invite People" (the task or activity to achieve this output). It's a fairly minor difference but worth sticking to in order to ensure the best results. We will move on to activities later in the planning process.

Scope Control

The bottom level of the PBS gives you the "Product Scope". This is the definition of all of the outputs that are expected from the project. This is a critical part of the planning process and you need to be very careful how you manage this. Although this book is about planning rather than execution of a project, it is important to emphasise that the Scope needs to be well controlled. Note that "Control" does not mean that the project team must necessarily resist change. There are often good business reasons which require a change. But any change must be managed. You will need to ensure that the change is the right thing to do, that the implications have been planned, that the stakeholders agree to the new plan and that everyone is aware of any change. Critically everyone, team and stakeholders, must always have the same understanding of what the product scope is at any point.

A few years ago I was working with a project team that had run into difficulties. The verification team had completed a set of tests and the tests were all failing. You would expect a few failures due to code errors or test errors, but a whole set of tests? Something was wrong. It was tracked down pretty fast. The features being tested weren't in the code. And they weren't in the code because they weren't in the product. In fact they had been taken out of the product but, crucially, no one had told the testing team. So the project had wasted time in writing tests and trying to work out why they were failing, which was wholly down to a failure in communicating a change to product scope.

Chapter 5 Exercise – Product Breakdown

Try building a Product Breakdown structure for yourself. Remember there is no "right" answer, this exercise is to learn about building a PBS, not about building a bicycle. Using a hierarchical layout, break down the top level requirement ("a bicycle", or if you are an expert on bicycles, "a mountain bike") to the level of defining parts that you could make or buy. This is not about the process of making or testing a bicycle, just a parts breakdown. An answer is at the end of the book.

Knowing what to do

So you've produced your Product Breakdown Structure. You now understand **what** you need to produce within your project (the product scope). The next stage is to look at **how** you are going to produce these items (the project activities). We've made that problem a lot easier by breaking things down into smaller, understandable pieces.

One mistake that people make is to introduce time at this point and start thinking about project schedule. They will typically introduce a grid structure of people and dates and start populating it with activities, looking something like below.

	Jan	Feb	Mar	Apr	May
Anne	Coding	Coding	Docs		
Bob	Coding	Coding			
Claire			Testing		
David					Release

Figure 16 - Grid-based timeline planning

So what is wrong with this approach? The problem is that you are starting with an expectation of the project duration and resourcing and so with a fixed number of cells, each representing a fixed amount of work. The natural tendency is to think of new tasks only until the cells are full and then to stop. Task identification is bounded by the perceived available space. The result is an idea of how to keep this many people busy for this many weeks, when what we want is an understanding of what is required to solve the problem which we have been given. By starting with a mind-set of the constraints we are potentially preventing finding a solution which achieves success.

> Scheduling activities reduces freedom for change and flexible thinking and should be done as late as possible in the planning.

Instead, you should think of a list of activities as just that – a list. At this stage there is no time, or even sizing information. You are trying to capture the complete set of work in the same way as you previously captured the complete set of outputs. Use any good list management tool to manage an activity list. Microsoft® Excel® is a good tool for this.

You are trying to achieve a list of activities covering every output which you identified in the PBS. While the PBS goes down to the level of understanding **what** you need to produce in detail and ensuring that no output is missed, the activity list looks at the work involved and understanding **how** each will be produced. Typically this means there will be several activities for each output, although that isn't a requirement – some outputs will be relatively trivial in nature.

Definition of Done

 A key point is to make sure that the activities are well understood. In particular, you want to know that when you have completed all of the activities, the output has been fully created. Why is this so critical and so frequently a failure area for project planning? If the activities to complete an output are not clear then the project may believe that it is "done" on the output when there is work remaining. This remaining work may be completely unknown, which will usually result in a defective output being generated. This might happen if testing were omitted and the output still integrated into the final product. However, even if the remaining work is known, perhaps if someone is aware that testing needs to be done, there is still a problem. Because the tracked activity is marked as complete, the plan for the project no longer has anyone assigned to do this work. This can lead to a hidden buildup of known (or unknown) work which can break a project. We need to ensure therefore that there is a clear "Definition of Done" which allows us to say that the completion of all the activities will complete the output.

I have seen several projects which suffered from issues around "Definition of Done". One significant case was a project which appeared to be going very smoothly. The project was moving through all of the design stages, completing reviews to check completion of all activities and appeared to be on track, with all reviews completed to schedule. Shortly after a review point, the team were replanning for the next section of the project and realised that there was a large amount of missed work – enough to set the project back several months. How had this been missed? At every review point activities were being marked as complete, even if reviews indicated significant rework. By closing down the planned activities as "done", but building up work which was not tracked, the project was eventually overwhelmed by incomplete activities. This is often referred to as "technical debt" – where a focus on "visible" features leads to a buildup of "invisible" issues, whether performance, defects or maintainability.

The diagram below shows a code development example. The output here is a code module. This could be a single activity, the activities can be grouped as the second level here – Coding, Reviewing etc., or may be broken down further to the third level. The key point here is that your activity list could have one activity, five, or fifteen. It doesn't matter which you do as long as you understand all of the work, you estimate for all of the work and you complete all of the work in each activity before marking the activity as complete. Typically larger outputs will need more breakdown to activities so don't treat every activity the same way.

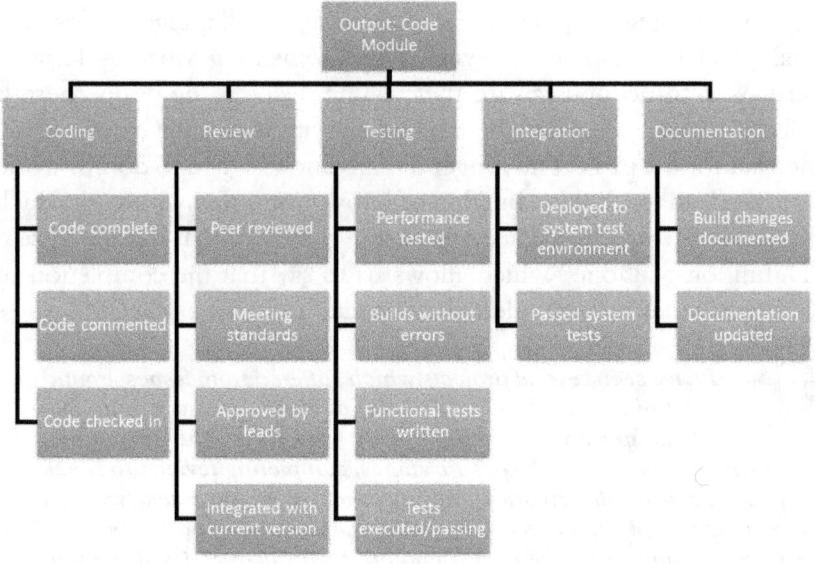

Figure 17 – Definition of Done

Chapter 6

Deterministic Estimation

How long is your string?

When talking about planning with teams, the area everyone seems most frightened of is task estimation. How can we know how long it will take to complete something until you've done it? And because teams are nervous, the approach they take to planning depends hugely on the culture of the organisation.

At one end of the spectrum, you have "political" organisations. In these everyone is frightened of making a mistake which might see them fired (or at least disadvantaged against their peers). In a political organisation, there is a strong incentive to "pad" estimates and to come out with numbers which are much higher than you believe the task will really take. That way you will deliver all of the tasks earlier than estimated and if the project fails, **it won't be your fault**. This approach, which seems to be prevalent in some cultures, leads to some writers assuming this will always be the case. Goldratt, in the Critical Chain methodology, recommends "take the current task estimates and cut them in half", which is a sound approach only if everyone is defensively doubling their estimates in a consistent and predictable way. However the world is not so straightforward. By contrast in a naïve organisation everyone may be so excited by the project that they instead under-estimate the complexity. This is not uncommon in technology projects. The ideal target is to have honest and realistic estimates and this may take some time and culture shift to achieve.

As with any culture change, you will need to reward the desired behaviour over time. This will need you to monitor results and encourage repeatable and accurate estimation. You are looking to make teams more accurate, not to see them complete under estimate more often. Although the latter is attractive, it again rewards a "padding" approach.

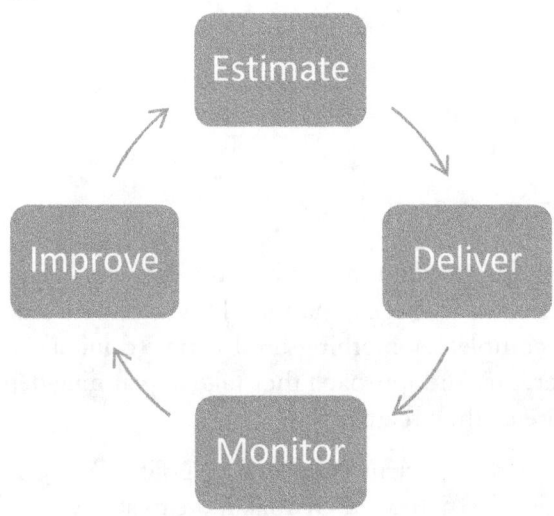

Figure 18 - Continuous improvement on estimation

The Rules of Estimation

Estimation is a group exercise. It uses the input of many to come to a consensus which is better than any individual can produce. When estimation is done well it is a great example of the "wisdom of crowds".

The "wisdom of crowds" goes back to Victorian statistician Thomas Galton. In 1906 he happened to be at a fair where there was a contest to guess the weight of an ox (no social media for entertainment in those days). Although no-one came out with the right answer, the average (mean) was almost exactly right (within 0.1%). This led to some of the concepts of sampling, where large data sets lead to low error rates.

Before you can have group estimation, you need to agree the rules. This makes sure that everyone means the same when they come out with a number. These are the basic rules that my team worked with.

1: Estimates are in terms of effort, not time. So a "1 week" estimate means "there is one week of work involved in completing this task".

2: The basic unit of estimating is a working day of effort, abbreviated to "d". This can also be expressed as a working week (1w=5d).

3: One working day (1d) represents the work which is normally completed in a day. Causes confusion so a bit more about this below.

4: Estimation is for a "typical team member". This one is also less straightforward than it sounds so there's a bit more about this one too.

One key factor in this approach is estimation in working days. A typical day will involve some meetings, some discussions and drinking some coffee. The number of hours being effective on a task list may be low (perhaps 3-4 in a day). However, averaging at the day level has proven a good approach to reliable estimating. This means that if we have a "1 week" task we would expect it to take about 1 week to deliver.

 There are two alternative approaches sometimes used rather than working days. These are to use "ideal time" or "story points". With an "ideal time" approach you estimate tasks in hours of focused activity. The meetings and distractions are excluded. So "40 hours" of work might take far more than a week to deliver. This works best for smaller activities, measured directly in hours. With a "story point" approach, you are giving relative sizes for tasks without directly stating how long these will take to deliver. Both approaches can be very effective in Agile environments through the use of "velocity", which calculates schedule based on past performance. These are however outside the scope of this book.

A complexity here is that we don't know who will be doing the work. We've only just got the task list sorted out, we do not know who our team is yet. So we're trying to estimate for a "typical" person. It's important not to assume experts – often there is an expert involved in estimating who will say "I could do this in a day". OK, maybe he or she could, but they can't solve every problem on the project personally. You know what you will be looking for as a team, so assume that skill level. If it's a task that you know you have to give to an expert because it's hard, assume an expert, but keep a note of that, or it will bite you later. And you'll need to make a reassessment of your assumptions when you do get assigned a team – many projects have been bitten by asking for a number of experienced team members and being assigned the same number of very inexperienced ones instead. Numbers are not everything.

The Tools of Estimation - Analogy

One of your biggest allies in estimation is analogy. How long did it take last time? Use this at all levels of your project and cross-check the data. If you have an output in your RBS, how long did it take to generate something similar last time? How much harder (or easier) is this one than the last one? Then look up and down the project. Compare specific activities – how long did the testing take last time, or the documentation. Work with your team to understand **why** it's different this time. Really think about complexity and don't let people be too optimistic on their timescales. If it took this long last time, it's likely to do so again unless you can point to what went wrong.

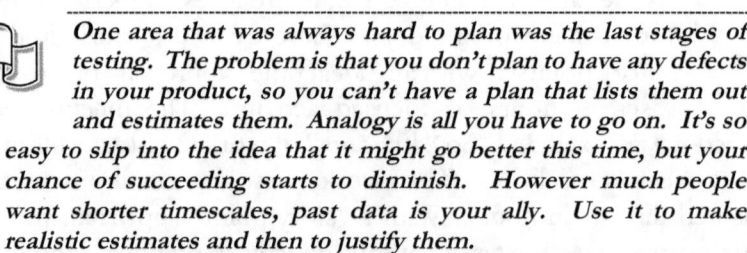

One area that was always hard to plan was the last stages of testing. The problem is that you don't plan to have any defects in your product, so you can't have a plan that lists them out and estimates them. Analogy is all you have to go on. It's so easy to slip into the idea that it might go better this time, but your chance of succeeding starts to diminish. However much people want shorter timescales, past data is your ally. Use it to make realistic estimates and then to justify them.

At a top level, we had some program managers who were great at analogous estimating. I can think of one in Texas and one in France (yes, I am aware that Texas, unlike France, is not a country, although perhaps the inhabitants are not) who would put in huge amounts of effort, cutting the project plan different ways, comparing with past projects for stages, technologies, however it could be subdivided, and seeing whether the relative sizes seemed right.

The Tools of Estimation - Decomposition

Your other ally here is decomposition. This is breaking down a big problem into smaller problems. It is well known that estimating a larger problem will tend to be less accurate than breaking it down into smaller problems and estimating these. If you've done a good job previously with identifying the outputs and breaking them down into activities, then you should be in a good position here. In particular, you'll be clear about your definition of done and so you'll know exactly what you're estimating for. However, it's good to know when to stop breaking tasks down. Not only does it take time to make the list longer, but past a certain point estimation stops becoming more accurate and starts becoming less accurate.

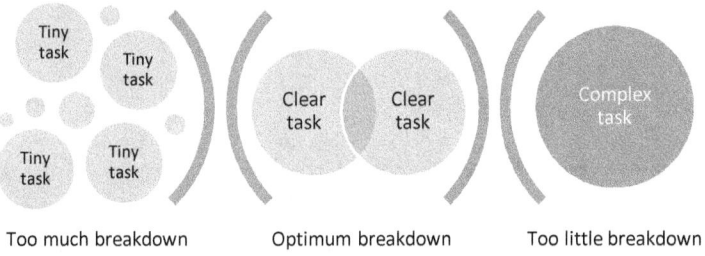

| Too much breakdown | Optimum breakdown | Too little breakdown |

Figure 19- Task breakdown

Imagine we have an output, a piece of code for example, which we think is around 10 weeks of work. We've used analogy - looking at other similar coding outputs in the past. We break this down into activities, let's say:

- 2 modules of coding, 1 week and 3 weeks
- Test writing, 2 weeks
- Testing and fixing bugs, 1 week
- Documentation, 3 days
- Release, 2 days

So overall the estimate is 8 weeks. By breaking this down into smaller elements we can be a little more confident in the numbers. But does that mean that breaking it down further would give us more accuracy? If we took the initial 1 week task and tried to split it into ten sub-tasks, what would happen? Firstly we might have immense trouble splitting this to such fine detail without actually doing the task. And secondly we would end up with very small subtasks. And there can be a reluctance to assign very small estimates to these. We might find that the ten sub-tasks were all estimated at a day each, pushing the total up to 2 weeks, simply because it is hard to visualise completing a task in a very small amount of time. So take care and watch for over-decomposition.

> Divide each difficulty into as many parts as is feasible and necessary to resolve it

This is a quote from Rene Descartes, the brilliant French philosopher, mathematician and logician. None the less valid for being stated 400 years ago. Estimation is a pragmatic activity - you need to break down activities as much as brings value, but don't break things down too far just to have something to do. It is possible to "over analyse" a problem

Gaining consensus

We want to involve a range of opinions and input. We want to ensure that everyone's past experience is used and we want to avoid Groupthink (as described earlier). How do we do this if we know that the team will influence each other? One approach is to keep everyone separate, give them a list of tasks and ask them for independent estimates. Then collate these together. This is the basis of a method called the "Delphi" technique (not sure it's a great name – the oracle at Delphi predicted the future, which is good, but famously in a cryptic and often misunderstood way). If the spread of estimates for a task is low, then the answer is likely to be a good estimate ("wisdom of crowds" again). If the spread is high, you need to find out why. It will probably be for one of two reasons:

> Different people have different interpretations of the activity. That's down to your "Definition of Done". You weren't clear enough what the activity actually is, and so different people give you different estimates. Go back, define more clearly and ask people again.

> Different people have different experiences. Though they have the same understanding of the activity, their past experience affects the outcome. You need to understand what their individual learnings may be.

Delphi as an approach is effective. Unfortunately it is also slow, and dull. By asking everyone independently it doesn't bring in team discussion until that final stage. So how can we make estimation a team activity but avoid Groupthink?

 There's a pretty good solution to this and it's called Planning Poker ™. Hang on, you may be saying, that's an Agile technique so shouldn't that be in the Agile book? Well, it's not really a technique specific to Agile Planning, but one that's generally applicable to any estimation situation. So, how does this approach work? You have a set of cards which represent effort estimates. Let's say you have the set below. Exact values used do vary, although the gaps always increase. The sequence is approximately based on Fibonacci numbers.

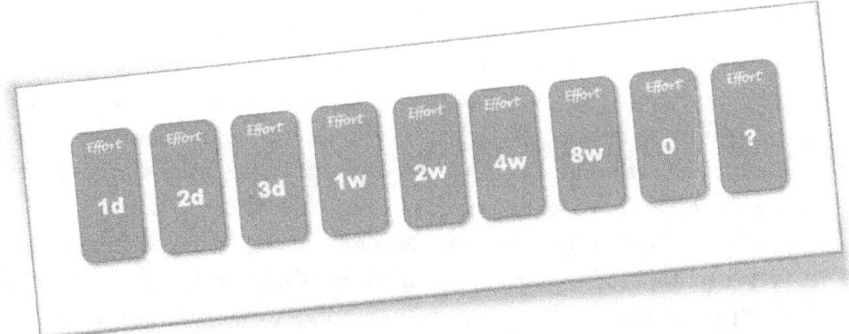

Figure 20 – Planning Poker™ cards

Each card has an effort estimate in days or weeks. The deck includes "0" (much less than a day) and "?" (I don't know). Each member of the team is given a set of cards. Then each activity is put up on a screen, and without any discussion of estimates beforehand, everyone picks **one** card and puts it **face down** in front of them. Finally, everyone turns the cards over, and there is a discussion about any differences of opinion. It is important to run the process rigorously with everyone choosing without being influenced by the other answers.

As you will see, this ticks all the estimation process boxes. It includes the whole team in the estimation process. But because the process is "blind" until the cards are revealed, there is no way for Groupthink to influence the answer. The variation inevitably leads to discussion and a final consensus on a good estimate for the task.

This was always a popular exercise on training courses, where we would try out Planning Poker on the course. It was always impressive (both as an observer and to the attendees) to see how much this sparked off dialogue about why people had chosen particular estimates. In a real project however you need to ensure that you have a supportive environment. Effective team inclusion will be killed if the first comment on the first task is "Don't be ridiculous, you're an idiot".

Where does time come in?

Up to this point the planning has focussed on Analysis. This is the breaking down of problems. We have taken the Requirements, broken them down into outputs, and then broken those down further into activities. And then we have looked at the activities and generated estimates for them. Now it's time to start on Synthesis – putting this together to make a picture of the project. This is the first point at which we start thinking about dates. Up to now the planning has been entirely about what we **need** to do, so we have avoided too much focus on the answer that people inevitably want. You should try and avoid too much discussion about desired end dates until the task estimation is complete.

We are looking at deriving a schedule. The starting point is that work, people and time are related by time being work divided by number of people. Of course anyone who has worked on projects knows that's a simplification, but let's work with it for now. What this simple formula gives us is a way to quickly get an idea of time from an activity list. We may have to replan with a changed scope, or changed team, and we need those answers quickly. A project schedule can be too slow.

Our working project schedules used for tracking progress were very detailed and managed in Microsoft® Project. This was effective as a tracking tool, but once you have a 4000 line project schedule with every detail assigned "just so", it was really slow to replan. You really don't want to drop in on a project manager and ask them to "just" try a replan with an extra person, as you risk getting a fairly robust reply. More critically you won't get a new schedule in less than a couple of days, which can be just too slow.

Chapter 6 Exercise – "MakeIt" Project Sizing

 Let's look at an example project which we will call "MakeIt". We'll use this in a few places to compare some numbers around estimation. It's a fairly simple project - we're planning for a stage in which we have a set of design tasks totalling 200 days and a set of documentation tasks totalling 100 days. All are independent of other tasks (so we don't have to wait for any task to complete). And we have a team of three designers (who can only do the design work), two authors (who can only do the documentation) and a lead who could do either design or documentation. We can show this as below.

Figure 21 – "MakeIt" Project Sizing Exercise

Let's use the basics above and consider how long this project would take, using work and people. An answer is at the end of the book.

Running this as a project

Dividing work by people to get time is a start, but it's not as simple as that. And a project which stops there will rapidly run into problems. The main issue that's being ignored is that not everything that happens is on your task list. We have said that you shouldn't account separately for meetings, coffee and all of the basics of office life. But what might be preventing your team from being in place and working on your project?

Firstly, you may not have been assigned all of your team's time to your project. They may have other responsibilities (such as line management) or (worse still) other projects. If a team member is split between two projects, it gives you only half a person. In reality it's probably less than that. A good principle is to try and have your team only on your project if you can, as time is always lost in context switching when people are on multiple projects. If you can't arrange that, try and agree which is their "main" project which gets the time when things get tough. Ideally it's yours…

Next, your team won't be in the building all of the time. They will be on leave, or on training (you were planning to send them on training, I hope). How much time is spent out of the office will vary by company and site, but a reasonable figure is that the team are available 85% of the time. This isn't time spent at project meetings or lingering at the water cooler, it's actually not being in the office.

Closely related to training is ramp-up time. Even if formal training isn't used, it will take time for team members to become effective with the tools and technology. Would you rather have one person for 12 weeks or twelve people for a week each? Intuitively you can see that you won't get much effective work from the second case.

Another major consideration is the work involved in managing a team. As soon as you have formed a team, there is work in making it run smoothly. Coaching, reviewing, meetings, discussions will take time if we want the team to head in the right direction and work smoothly. There's no easy answer exactly how much time this needs, but we studied this and concluded that a well-run team takes about 15% of the team size in management effort. This could be concentrated in a few individuals (project managers for example), or distributed through a hierarchy of engineering leads, or typically both, but it's not on the task list.

Let's take a moment to consider the statement above as it's quite shocking to some people. A 15% management overhead means that if you have an 8 person team you will "lose" a whole person to manage the team. That work could be focussed in a project manager, or it could be distributed across the team (the agile "self-organising team" concept. But typically it falls on a project lead. This individual is often the expert, and is heavily planned in the task list as he or she can deliver fast and well. But they are also relied on to run the team. Inevitably this leads to tension and potentially delivery failure.

I recall one project, where we were developing a system component. There was a ten person team and the project was running behind schedule. We were looking at how to bring it back on track. There was little option to rescope. Could we put more people on the project? In the end the solution was quite radical – we took people off the project. By cutting the team from 10 to 7, removing the least experienced, we freed up significant time from the lead engineer. This meant he had time to work on project tasks, which he could deliver fast and with low errors. With hard work all round, the project pulled back on track.

The last area on the list is operational activities. There are some items which need to be done over the length of the project rather than being a fixed amount of work.

- Supporting customers or an external community.
- Running infrastructure – build and test systems for example.
- Running the office.

The size of these will vary but they all scale with the length of the project.

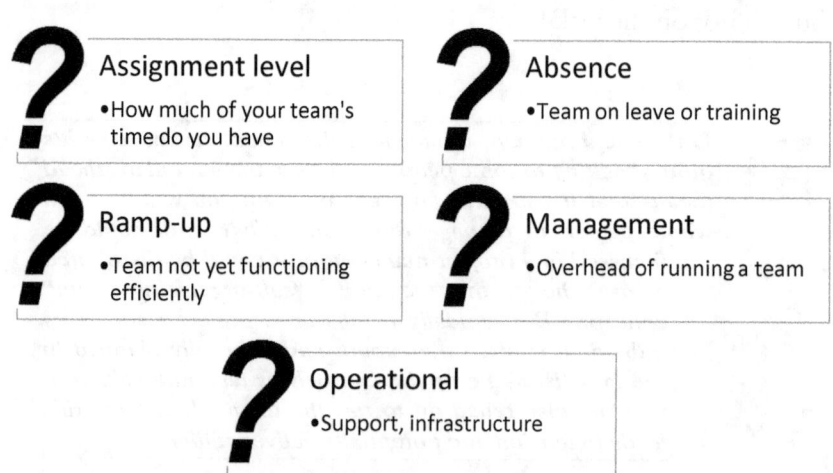

Figure 22 - Key overheads

Chapter 6 Exercise – "MakeIt" Product Overheads

So what is the impact of these overheads? Let's go back to the same problem. We still have a set of design tasks totalling 200 days and a set of documentation tasks totalling 100 days. And we have a team of three designers, two authors and a lead who could do either design or documentation. But now we have 15% leave & vacation, a management overhead of 15% and 25% of someone's time on support.

Figure 23 – "MakeIt" Project Overheads Exercise

How long would this project take, estimated with overheads? A worked answer is at the end of the book.

Let's compare the two exercises. The first, just looking at the task list, gave us an estimated duration of 10 weeks. By considering the overheads involved in running this as a project, we realise that we will need 15 weeks to deliver this. There is more to a project than simply a task list and you will generally see a significant increase in required schedule when overheads are considered. Make sure you plan for these early and avoid setting an expectation of early delivery in the minds of your stakeholders.

Successful plans include realistic estimates for the overall project environment.

Scenarios and negotiation

OK, this is the crunch point of the planning. You've worked hard on this plan and you believe in it. You know what you need to deliver (the outputs), you know how you can deliver it (the activities) and you know how long it will take for a given team (project sizing). You understand the requirements and you know that this plan maps well to the success criteria. Hurrah! Doesn't that mean all the work is done?

All too often, however, teams fail at the final hurdle, the negotiation stage. What you have so far is a "scenario". It represents a combination of scope, team and timescales that you think is achievable. But it's not a plan you can deliver until you have agreement that this is the "right" plan. And this is where conflict typically appears. Not every stakeholder will want the same scenario. A resource manager may want to keep level of work down, while a marketing manager may want to keep scope up.

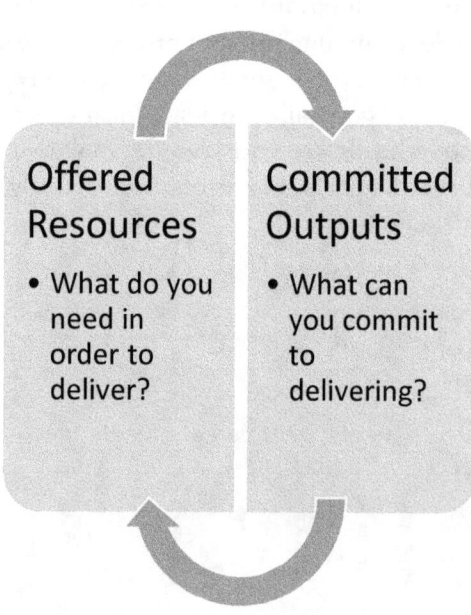

Figure 24- Negotiation

You cannot make everyone happy. You are in a negotiating situation and are looking for the best "win" for all. And that's a situation where many project leaders don't feel comfortable. But you have some advantages. The key one is that you've done the planning. You have a breakdown of the scenario with all the work and assumptions. And you have it in a very flexible form. So as you negotiate, you can respin scenarios with ease and elegance.

"What if we drop that feature, and give me 8 weeks of another designer? That will give you this new scenario." Speed to turn around new and confident scenarios as you zero in on the agreed one is critical here. If it takes a week of replanning and to respond to a suggestion you will never get out of the mire of the negotiation stage.

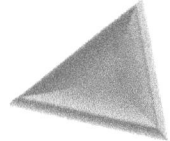 What are your areas of freedom? You are mostly trading between Work (how many people do you have available), Scope (what do you have to produce) and Schedule (when will you deliver it). This is the famous "Iron Triangle" of deterministic project management.

You may need to work hard to gain agreement. When negotiating on plan scenarios, imagination is needed. There may be several available options. Phased deliveries let people get some of what they want when they want it, and all of what they want a bit later. Early releases let you offer features first and quality later. As the scenario becomes more complex, make sure that everyone knows what they are getting.

An example was a new microprocessor development. This one was going to be risky because it used a new way of communicating around the chip (a "bus" in chip-speak) which was being developed elsewhere in the company. Now this key dependency meant delay, added risk of rework and added testing time. No way would the development hit its aggressive schedule. How would we deal with this? We went back to the requirements and the customers. The customers who wanted the early dates liked the new features, but they didn't have time to build in the new bus in their first releases. So the project was replanned with a first release that took out the new bus, so removing test time and risk, and pushed this to a later release. This held the aggressive delivery schedule with no reduction in customer value. Full marks for creative planning and an understanding of the concept of "minimal viable product" – what really are those "must have" items?

What do you need out of the negotiation stage? There's a key checklist of outcomes. Don't leave this stage until you can tick them all. It is incredibly tempting to run ahead without these, but as in the example of Sydney Opera House, you can get badly bitten if you lack agreement. Sometimes you may need to get your team started on some low risk items, but you need to stay clear that you are still negotiating until you have all of these ticked.

An understood problem
• Everyone agrees the product scope

An achievable plan
• You are confident in the plan that is being agreed

Commitment from the team
• Everyone agrees this is the right plan and is achievable

Commitment from suppliers
• Whatever you need, your suppliers agree with the plan.

Happy stakeholders
• All stakeholders believe they are getting good value

Figure 25 – Checklist of planning outcomes

Trust the planning work. If you've put in all of that work, don't sign up to something that you have proved is impossible.

Chapter 7

Deterministic Scheduling

Scheduling is coming fairly late in the planning process. This is a basic part of the approach that we are taking. We have focussed so far on understanding **what** we have to make, and then **how** we can make it. We can even get a fair level of agreement on **when,** and **if** it is agreed. So what is scheduling and where does it become involved?

> *To many people, scheduling is what project planning is all about. I've met a few people (who should know better) who seem to think planning and scheduling are the same thing. I know that there's a tradition of blaming Microsoft® for all of our woes, but in this case maybe there's some justification. With a strong market presence for Microsoft® Project, it's easy for planners to throw their ideas into such a tool and be presented with a schedule from the start.*

It's quite hard to find a definition of what scheduling means in projects but the dictionary one below is a fair starting point.

> *Scheduling: Arrange or plan (an event) at a particular time.*
>
> *Oxford English Dictionary*

Up to now we have been thinking mostly about work. We have brought in an estimate of dates for key milestones. Scheduling brings in time at the individual tasks level. In particular we have to consider three factors which we have not worked with to date.

- Assignment – who will be performing each activity?
- Dependencies – do certain events (internal or external) have to happen before an activity?
- Sequencing – in what order should the activities happen?

We can see that this is adding a fair amount of detail. That's why we haven't recommended you did this earlier. If you have carefully assigned every task to someone and your team size changes, it's going to take some work for you to build a new schedule. So why do we bother scheduling at all? Why not just stick with our task list? Well, some projects do just that. Agile projects will typically order the task list but not build a schedule at all and not try and define when each task will be done. But if you suggested that to someone in the construction industry it would probably sound a little shocking (the world is probably not yet ready for Agile building practices, but maybe there are some out there). Why the difference of approach? It is down to understanding the value you are getting from scheduling. Your approach to scheduling should be based on its value to you, while it often seems to be because "a Gantt chart is expected".

Building a chain, link by link

The first and most critical reason for scheduling is to understand and manage dependencies. A "dependency" is an activity which requires the completion of another activity before it can be performed. To the purist, there are some details here (does it need the earlier activity to complete before it starts or before it finishes) but in general we assume that if B depends on A, it means that A must be complete before we start on B. Thus far we've suggested that Work divided by People is a good way to derive Time. In an environment that is very driven by dependencies that's not going to work. It's no good saying that you can deliver the project in 8 weeks if something prevents you starting until 12 weeks' time. So your starting point for your schedule is capturing and understanding external dependencies. These may affect the whole flow of your project so even if there are not many dependencies make sure you understand what they are and what depends on them.

Projects are often structured in stages and this sets up effective dependencies. All the activities in the first stage must generally be completed before those in the next stage. Stages may be defined by feature set or quality level of the output. When planning at this point, it is sensible to assume that **all** stage 1 activities will be completed, leading to a release or review point, followed by commencing stage 2.

However, when the project is running, a degree of pragmatic flexibility is needed and there may be some "blending" of stages to ensure the whole team isn't stalled by a single overrunning activity.

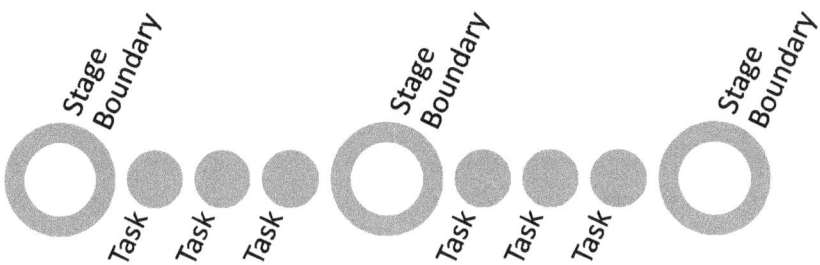

Figure 26- Stages and tasks

You have looked at external dependencies and the top level stages. Now you can push down to the next level and start looking at dependencies between tasks. This is again an area where pragmatism is key. An inexperienced project manager, especially one with a scheduling tool such as Microsoft® Project, may build a cross-linked mesh of dependencies which makes a project hard to read and harder still to maintain. What you should be looking for is **strong** dependencies which will affect the flow of the project and which will need managing or prioritisation. Most importantly, dependencies are not about people but about work. At this stage we have not yet decided who will do which work. When we decide that Anne will do task X and then task Y, that is not a dependency, it is a decision on sequencing. We could just have easily have decided that Anne would do Y and then X, or that Anne would do X and Bill would do Y. Dependencies should also be between tasks, and not task groupings (some tools call these "summary tasks"). Saying "all the group A tasks must be done before any of the group B tasks" may make your schedule look neat but can artificially restrict your planning freedom.

> Dependencies should only be about hard constraints between tasks or with external inputs. This keeps the schedule manageable.

Assessing the Critical Path

Once you have established the dependencies it is useful to have a look at the Critical Path. The Critical Path Method, often abbreviated to CPM, was developed in the 1950s and the approach taken has been revolutionised by scheduling software, but the basic principle is quite simple. Where a project has a set of dependencies, this reduces your ability to reorder tasks freely. If you must do task A then B then C, your project can never be shorter than the total of the times to do these tasks. When you are planning, this sequence "the Critical Path" becomes the backbone of your plan while other tasks D, E and F can be fitted round this. And when running your project you should try and ensure that the tasks on your critical path do not lengthen, while the others **may** be able to delay or lengthen without delaying the project. An example is below, although a real project will be much more complex and identifying the critical path could be a real challenge in the days before scheduling software.

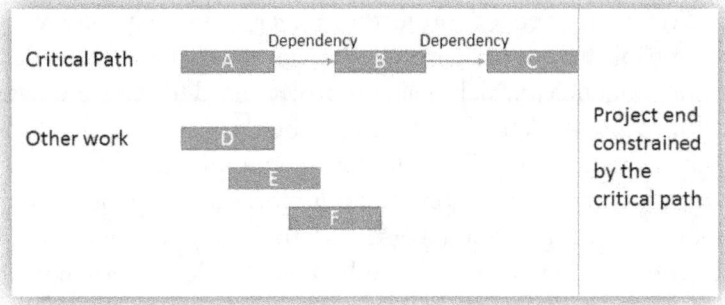

Figure 27 – Critical Path Analysis

Critical Path Analysis is a valuable tool and it's worth understanding the key points about the Critical Path. Which tasks are on the Critical Path? How dominant is the Critical Path? In a project with strong dependencies there may be one clear sequence and little "other work". But in another project, much of the work might be able to be reordered and the project is more about getting all the work completed.

The CPM approach also has its limitations, and these have become clearer over the years. Despite the name it is important to remember that CPM does not take account of the importance of tasks – it is about the criticality in the current schedule, not to the project as a whole. Don't let teams get confused into thinking that a task that is not on the Critical Path is not critical to complete. Most projects will try and avoid gaps in the work so, unless the project is very heavily dominated by external dependencies, will likely end up with multiple critical paths. And as we will see later, CPM is based on a very stable and deterministic planning approach. As we introduce Uncertainty, Critical Path Analysis needs to be rethought to some degree.

Who will do what?

The next stage is to start working out who will do which work. By now you have your agreed set of tasks, you have these split into stages and you understand the key dependencies and whether there is a strong critical path. We've got a long way through the process before we do this and for a good reason. Assignment takes a lot of thought and adds a lot of detail so this is really the point at which your project starts to lose flexibility. If you take a whole schedule and assign all the tasks you have a schedule which can be hard to maintain. Maybe you need to do this or maybe you can adopt something more flexible. In some cases the "assign to teams" approach may be appropriate where you assign tasks to a team of similarly skilled people without the need to say exactly who will do each task. This can be decided closer to the time. This is really the approach taken in Agile planning where assignment is typically done only when the task is commenced. But more typically you will need to do some assignment at the planning stage. This is to ensure that you not only have enough people for the work, but have the right people and the right skills. Otherwise it's too easy to find that the numbers add up in your plan, but you have been given coders when you want testers, or graduates when you want experts.

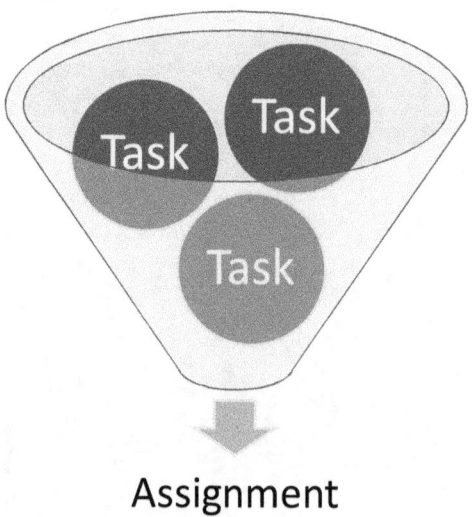

Figure 28 - Assigning tasks

Start the process of task assignment by looking at the tasks that can only be done by one person. The Lead, the resident expert, there's always some tasks that you know who will do them, so your schedule is going to need to make sure they are free. The next consideration is which tasks are "hard". There's a lot of evidence that individual skill can make substantial differences on how long tasks take to complete. Ratios as high as three to one have been suggested on the work to complete a task for an inexperienced team member against an experienced one. So try and identify those tasks which will benefit from experience and start to put your best people on them. You rarely have the luxury of a whole team of experts, so use the experience you have wisely.

For the remaining tasks, who does which task still benefits from some thought. Work with the team and the line management to decide what may be best. One major factor is the balance of specialization against rotation. It can take time for people to learn new tools or technologies. We call this "ramp-up" time. So keeping someone on related tasks may be efficient as they build up learning. But remember that past a certain point this may be demotivating, especially if it is a low status task. Also remember that if only one person understands that technology you are building up some Risk. What if they leave or they are ill? Can you still build and release your product if the "build system expert" leaves? And are you doing enough to keep him or her, or just throwing them tasks because he or she is good at them?

Think about how the task assignments can build a better team. Some tasks involve close co-working. Two designers working on the same code, or a designer and a tester, will work best if they can communicate. Ideally this means choosing co-located people. Or people who have worked together before and know each other. It doesn't just take time to learn new tools, it also takes time to build and rebuild teams. How about developing a new team member in an area you will need in the next project. Or maybe you need to build up a team member's confidence by assigning them a low risk task. Or perhaps you decide they are right to take on more responsibility and give them the keystone of the project.

Working within your means

By this point you have most of the hard work done on the schedule. You understand the real dependencies and you have a good idea of whom you would like to do what. However most of your tasks aren't scheduled yet because typically they don't have dependencies. Perhaps there are ten tasks to be done between milestones A and B but they could be done in any order. Levelling is the process of coming out with an achievable option. Not the only option (we could do these tasks in any order) but one that is possible, because no-one is assigned to do more work than they are able to. You need to be very aware of who you have on the project, for how long and how much of their time in order to make this achievable. Depending on your tools and the size of the project, levelling may be more or less of a challenge, but you need to be confident that your schedule is accurately levelled. It's easy to have a schedule that looks convincing and hits the dates, but has everyone working 10 day weeks. And remember about Overheads. Your critical people will be managing the team, so you may have less of their time than you had hoped.

One major learning was how easy it is to expect too much of the lead engineer. With inexperienced leads or planners you would see plans that showed the expert completing many of the planned tasks. But it never worked that way. The lead has to do just that – lead. He or she is accountable for the team, not just for his own work, plans that expected him or her to execute on tasks were rarely successful. Remember the overheads.

Your final commitment

You have your complete plan, and have reached the final step. Make some final checks on the schedule. You need to be sure your stakeholders are happy with what your plan. You need to be confident that your suppliers can get you everything that you need when you expect it. And then you commit to your plan. It stops being "a scenario" and becomes "the baseline plan".

> *Baseline: starting point used for comparisons.*
>
> ***Oxford English Dictionary***

Your "baseline" is a record of the agreed plan. This includes what Requirements have been agreed, what resources and budget you have been given, what outputs you expect to produce, what tasks you expect to perform and when, and what you have committed to deliver. It is a full snapshot of the plan. Not only is this a record of what has been agreed and against which success will be judged, it is also the data against which you will track progress later.

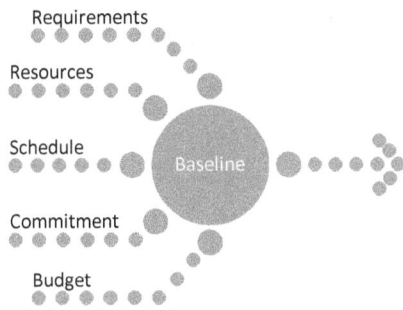

Figure 29 - Setting a baseline

> *It's easy to assume that everyone will just remember what was agreed. However, this is often not the case. It can have been a long negotiation to get the plan finally agreed so make sure there is a clear record. You don't want to prevent change for a good reason, but change needs to be managed. I have sat in review meetings where you realise that everyone has a slightly different idea of what the project has agreed to do and when. That's not usually a great sign for a project. At this point it's a good idea to call "halt" and maybe go round the table and get everyone to state their "version of the truth". It can be quite informative.*

Chapter 7 Exercise - Scheduling

Scheduling has been transformed by the introduction of scheduling software. However scheduling software is so powerful and automated there is a risk that the users forget what it is trying to achieve. There is no better way to think through the process than to try some manual scheduling. It also helps you appreciate just what the tools are doing for you.

In this exercise, assume you have identified and estimated the tasks below, and have gathered some information from the teams on the dependencies between the tasks. You have three team members – Alex, Bill and Cindy – and you have only 50% availability for Bill. You do not need to consider any overheads, let's assume that's included in the 50% availability figure.

ID	Task	Effort	Notes and Constraints
1	Coding function A	2w	This would only be 8 days effort if it's Bill
2	Coding function B	1w	
3	Testing function A	2w	Coders test their own code
4	Testing function B	2w	
5	Integrate into system	1w	Could be before or after testing. Only Cindy can do this task.
6	Demo new features	2w	After integration, can be before testing
7	User testing with new features	2w	Needs function testing first
8	Release packaging	1w	Only Cindy can do release
9	Code review	1w per function	You can't review your own code

For this exercise you should convert this task list into a project schedule, which you can draw as a Gantt chart. Start by thinking about the Critical Path and its implications and move on to assigning individuals to tasks. A worked example is at the end of the book

Chapter 8

Introducing Uncertainty

Chapter 8 Exercise - Uncertainty

In the first chapters we invested a lot of time in a deterministic planning process. It looked pretty good and we came out with a complete plan. Take a few minutes to think about what might have been missing. In a real project environment, what are we are trying to achieve with uncertainty planning, beyond what deterministic planning gains us?

Planning in an uncertain world

In the previous chapters we looked at deterministic planning. This is built around a clearly defined process of defining the problem, identifying the work, estimating the work and then synthesising this into a plan for the project as a whole. This is similar to a child's building blocks, perhaps a tool such as Lego®. You picture the blocks as being fixed and square edged. Unfortunately project teams quickly discover that planning isn't like that. You don't know all of the answers so we can have a discrepancy between planning, where we try and decide the best path forwards, and uncertainty, where we don't have all of the information.

> *Plan*: A detailed proposal for doing or achieving something
> *Uncertain*: Not able to be relied on; not known or definite
>
> *Oxford English Dictionary*

 Combining the two we have the idea of "Uncertainty Planning". This is how to make decisions about what to do in the future in a situation in which not everything is known. This is an environment which many project teams find challenging and uncomfortable. They may have learned process and techniques for Deterministic Planning, and sometimes it's the experts at planning who find uncertainty hardest. There is surprisingly little discussion about how to manage the imprecision of real projects. In particular we need to understand how to protect the project against what **might** go wrong. Often teams are just unaware this is needed as part of the planning process.

Case Study – an uncertain journey

Travel by train

At one point I had to travel regularly between offices in Cambridge and Sheffield in the UK. For those less than familiar with the UK, that looks as shown on a map of the UK. I would choose to make the journey by train. Now, it's a fairly inconvenient journey as it involves three trains and a certain amount of waiting on cold platforms. I had to tell people when I'm going to arrive, which means building a plan of when I would arrive. But how would I know which trains to take? Of course I would consult a phone app which gives me train timetables. The phone app gave me the train times below. This became my plan and I expected to arrive at 8:56 in Sheffield.

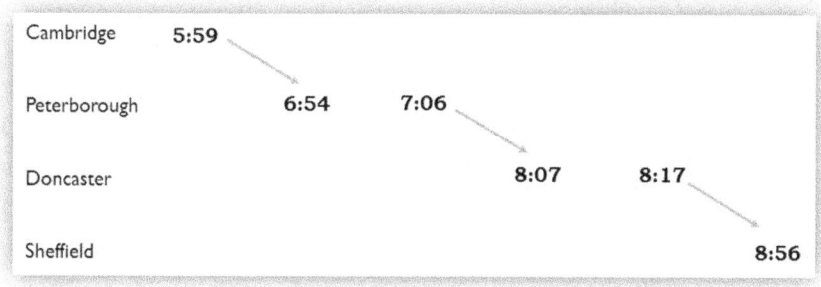

Figure 30 – A train timetable

What happened?

As I travelled the route regularly, I found there are other trains apart from the ones I had been told about, travelling the same routes. In particular, I could sometimes catch an earlier train at two of the stations, getting me to Sheffield nearly ten minutes earlier. But there was no record of this on the timetable suggested on my phone. Why not? Was this just an error? I wanted to be early, so surely a plan that means I arrive at 8:47 has to be better than a plan that means I arrive at 8:56.

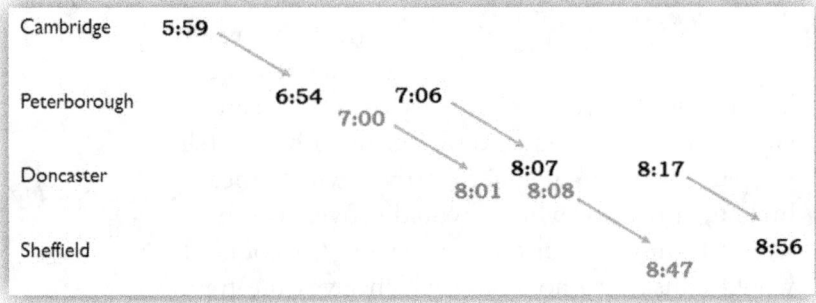

Figure 31 – An alternative train timetable

Why did this happen?

If the first train was a little late, I wouldn't catch the earlier option. I only managed to catch it about one trip in three. The train timetable therefore has an option of telling me the 8:56 arrival time, which I would achieve 90% of the time, or the 8:47 arrival time, which I would achieve 30% of the time. If I were given 8:47 as an arrival time, and arrived at 8:56 I would feel that I was "late" and might miss an appointment. As a result, the app elects for a plan which you can rely on and it does this by building in a rule that you always allow ten minutes between trains.

What can we learn?

If we publish a plan which said that we would arrive at 8:47, there would be a 30% chance that we would be on time. If we publish a plan that says that we would arrive at 8:56, there is a 90% chance that we would be on time. We choose the later time because the value in a stable plan is greater than in an early, but unreliable date. This is a key driver to uncertainty management and is far from intuitive. When working with deterministic planning you are usually looking for the earliest date.

> A plan which can be relied on has more value to the business than an unreliable plan which suggests an earlier delivery.

What do we mean by Uncertainty?

If we look at the train Case Study, we don't know how long each stage will take. When the timetable says one journey runs from 5:59 to 6:54, that's a best estimate. There will be two main factors that impact a train journey. One is that, as we all know, things may go seriously wrong. There may be an equipment failure, a shortage of trains or a problem with weather. These are significant single events where we can point to a cause and an effect. The other case is the cumulative effect of many small factors – how long did a door take to close, how many people got into which carriage, how mobile were they? There's an effect, but no single cause. The first of these is what is termed "Risk" in project management – the fourth of my "four horsemen". For Risk there is a cause which we can attack to make our project more likely to succeed. Uncertainty is the second case, the cumulative effect of many small factors. Typically Risk has lower probability but could have high impact (think of equipment failure on the train line), while Uncertainty has high probability but low impact, as below.

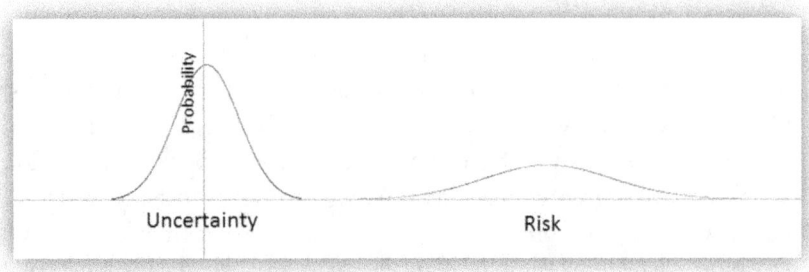

Figure 32 – Uncertainty and Risk

We can make an effort to understand the level of uncertainty but we probably can't do much to affect the root causes. Train companies run lots of trains so they have a pretty good idea of the spread of train journey durations. And that's the basis for their "ten minutes between trains" rule.

Can Uncertainty Management help?

It is easy to believe that uncertainty is a problem that cannot be effectively managed. Many project managers see it as being unmanageable or being a subject for experience or "gut feel". But my own experience is that you can see the difference between teams that manage uncertainty well, and those that struggle.

When you are working with a team that can handle the level of uncertainty, everyone is working together and it feels as below:

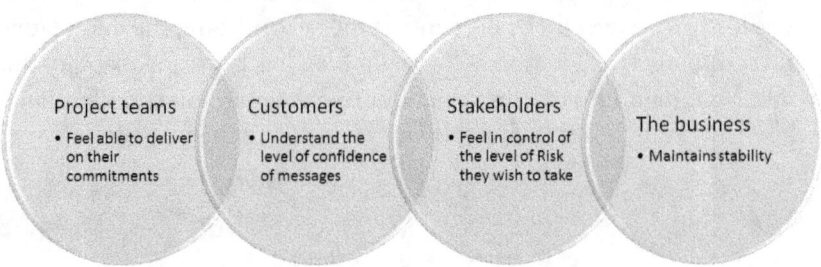

And when they cannot manage, it leads to breakdown and confusion.

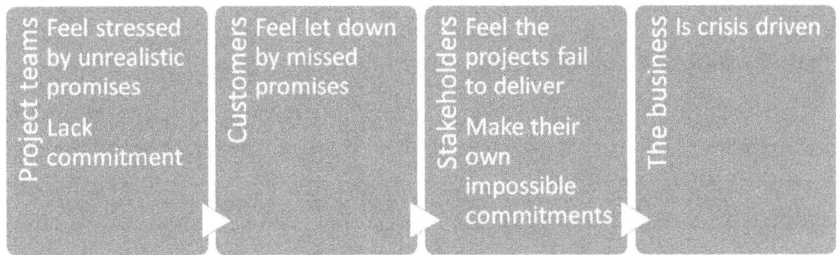

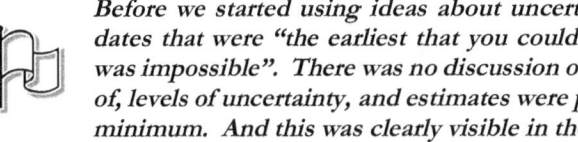

Before we started using ideas about uncertainty, plans gave dates that were "the earliest that you couldn't actually prove was impossible". There was no discussion of, or management of, levels of uncertainty, and estimates were pared down to the minimum. And this was clearly visible in the team's ability to deliver to schedule. If we looked at the dates planned at the start of the development stage of the project, the teams were hitting them about 10% of the time. Yes, 10%. And these were very competent teams, it's just that the culture and the planning failed to take into account the high uncertainty environment and the teams would overcommit. After introducing some uncertainty techniques and after 2 years work with the teams on changing the culture, on-time delivery reached 80% relative to initial plans and above 90% when formal change management was taken into account (resetting targets for significant scope change for example).

How can we capture uncertainty?

Three point Estimation

In an earlier chapter we looked at task estimation in a deterministic environment. When we have a higher level of uncertainty we need to capture the data to allow us to assess and manage the uncertainty. So when you work with the team to obtain task estimates you need to gain more than a single estimate. The usual approach taken is three point estimation. In this method, for each task you produce a "most likely" estimate and "best case" and "worst case" estimates. As with all estimation you need the team to understand what these mean. The "most likely" estimate, as its name suggests, is the amount of work which the task is expected to take and would be the single estimate given in a deterministic planning approach. The "best case" is how much work is involved if all goes well, and the "worst case" if all goes badly. Clearly some pragmatism is needed to ensure that "worst case" does not include a major multi-day power outage (for example). Remember we are looking at Uncertainty – if we discover a specific event that might cause a really significant lengthening of a task we would handle that through Risk Management. A general rule is to assume that "best case" and "worst case" represent a 10% probability.

So for example, a team may estimate as follows. The task to test a new function is most likely to take 4 days, but could complete in 3 days if the task went well or might take as long as 7 days if the function was at the top end of typical defect rates.

Three point estimation is a key input to project data, but there are variant approaches to be considered, depending on team experience.

Figure 33 - Three Point Estimation

Two point Estimation

In many cases it is seen that the uncertainty is quite asymmetric. It is unlikely that the task will take much less time, but it could take substantially longer. This seems to be typical of development environments where most tasks run fairly smoothly but unanticipated problems could occur in some cases. However, the possibility of unexpected benefits is less likely. This means that "best case" estimates are often little less work, but worst-case estimates may be significantly larger than "most likely" estimates. This leads to the conclusion that the "best case" estimates may not gain you significant information and on pragmatic principles, teams should focus on two pieces of data – "most likely" and "worst case" estimates for tasks.

So in the example above a simpler estimate could be as follows. The testing task is most likely to take 4 days, but might take as long as 7 days. Discarding the "best case" estimate saves us some time, and loses little useful data. However, note that the "most likely" effort is unchanged. This is a realistic estimate, not a "best case" one.

Figure 34 - Two Point Estimation

Rating tasks

There is not inconsiderable skill involved in three point (or even two point) estimation. Some teams lack the experience to come out with these estimates. You will need to spend a little time coaching and practicing with them and building up the team capability. A good tool for doing this development is to start with "rating" tasks. Instead of producing three point estimates, teams can assign "red", "amber" or "green" to each task, representing "high uncertainty", "medium uncertainty" and "low uncertainty" tasks. These can then be converted into typical "best case" and "worst case" figures based on suitable values for the project type. Feeding these numbers back to the team lets them see what numbers are appropriate and helps them be more prepared for next time.

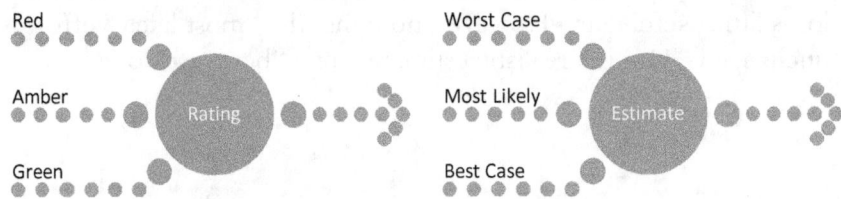

Figure 35 – Rating tasks

The projects with which I was working were a fairly high uncertainty environment, and typical values were as below. As you can see this is a long way from the deterministic planning case where exact work values are known.

Green tasks were highly predictable and had a typical "best case" of 90% and a worst case of 120% of the "most likely" estimate.

Amber tasks were innovative but moderate uncertainty such as design tasks and had a typical "best case" of 75% and a worst case of 150% of the "most likely" estimate.

Red tasks were high uncertainty such as testing tasks and had a typical "best case" of 50% and a worst case of 200% of the "most likely" estimate

So in the example above the team might estimate the testing task as a high uncertainty "red" task which is most likely to take 4 days, suggesting a "best case" of 2 days and a "worst case" of 8 days.

Planning Poker™ and Uncertainty

Planning Poker remains a great approach when collecting uncertainty data. You can get the team to estimate twice – once for "most likely" and once for "worst case" (this is a place where also getting "best case" data may just be too much work). Or you can look at the spread of responses and use this as an indication of "worst case" values. As an approach it's probably not quite as good as asking for both values but you always have to balance this with the need to keep the team involved and focussed. A bored team that is just going through the motions will never produce good data.

Chapter 9

Planning for Uncertainty

How can we effectively manage Uncertainty? In the last chapter we looked at capturing uncertainty and we need to know where the uncertainty in the project lies. But what can we do about it? We have already said that Uncertainty, unlike Risk, is built of a myriad of small effects. There is no single cause to mitigate and so you can rarely directly attack the problem. Instead, what you need to do is to ensure that your plan is robust enough. Thinking back to the example of train travel, you can help people on and off trains, blow whistles and shout "stand clear of the doors", all in an attempt to make the trains run to time, but you still need to allow time between changing trains.

The uncertainty tool

The basic tool for managing uncertainty is a "buffer". Although the term is used in project management it is hard to find a clear definition of what is meant by this. Generically a buffer is some free space or capacity which prevents one item affecting another nearby item. For example a "buffer state" is a small, uninvolved country between two rival countries which prevents either one interfering with the other. In a project environment we can consider a buffer as below:

> *Buffer - An available but unplanned capacity of time, cost and/or work added in to a plan to limit the impact of planning uncertainty*

By "buffer" we mean any extra capacity which we are holding in reserve to cover the uncertainty in the plan. This can use **any** of the three main planning parameters. You can have a Scope buffer, where some parts of the scope are optional and can be dropped if tasks overrun, a Work buffer, where some of the team are not assigned to planned tasks, or a Schedule buffer, where the committed end date is later than the deterministic plan date. Or a combination of these. Any of these three approaches will mean that you have some ability to deal with uncertainty. In the train example above there is a **schedule** buffer of ten minutes between trains. Some of this buffer will be used up if a train is late but the presence of the buffer prevents the late train impacting the overall plan. This is the form of buffering which is probably most familiar to people. In this book we will focus on schedule buffers as the buffering approach used. Scope buffers by contrast are the normal approach for Agile planning. Work buffering is not generally used as you rarely have the option of unused team members, although there are some areas where it can be used (for example assigning a contractor budget to be used if needed).

Implicit buffering

Any project manager soon learns that plans can overrun. They will develop their own approach to dealing with this. Many project teams respond by increasing the estimate for each task. If we have a task that we think will take 5 days, but it might overrun a little, why not call it a 7 day task? This is what is known as "implicit buffering", where the allowance for overrun is included in each task in a hidden form. Is there anything wrong with this implicit buffering approach? Unfortunately the evidence suggests that this doesn't lead to the most efficient projects. Imagine we do call that 5 day task a 7 day task. It's likely the team will take 7 days to deliver. Now imagine we have ten of these tasks in a row. We have increased the total from 50 days to 70 days, allowing 20 extra days in case something goes wrong. Let's say we've done 9 of the tasks. At 7 days each, we've taken 63 days and we have only 2 spare days for the last task. If this is the one that overruns substantially, we're late because we threw away all that buffering.

Explicit buffering

The solution is **explicit** buffering. Instead of adding buffer on to a task, it is collected at one or more points in a project. The buffer is visible in the plan and of enough size to have a good probability of delivering. In the example above, instead of adding 2 days to each task, we can add all 20 days as a buffer. Now each task is restored to being 5 days each, so the team is focussed on their estimate. The buffer is collected at the end so that it is unused until a task overruns, when a portion of the buffer is consumed to maintain the fixed end date. The buffer represents both an increase in schedule and in cost/effort. The difference in approach is shown below.

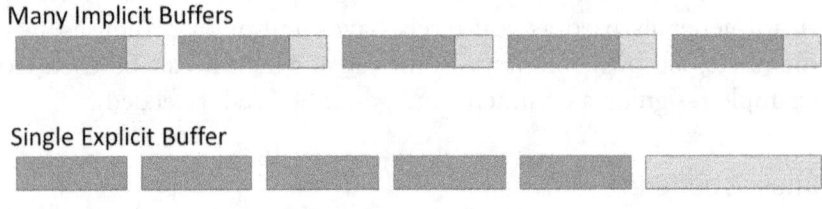

Figure 36 – Explicit buffering

From my experience the main challenge here is not teaching the approach. Teaching does need some work and as we will see there are some areas where training and consistency are important. The challenge is that explicit buffering is a big cultural shift. A good planning culture is built on teams being enabled to succeed on their projects due to realistic and achievable plans. Initially I had several managers state that "aggressive" schedules "motivate teams" and that buffering makes them "lazy". But over time we moved from project reviews removing or slashing buffers to reviews that questioned why buffers were missing or smaller than historic data suggested. Eventually the buffering approach became part of the structure and even language of our projects.

Where do you place buffers?

We need to be using buffers effectively to protect the **schedule** of the project. Typically a project is separated into a sequence of "stages", where each stage indicates a level of progress whether increasing functionality or increasing quality. Each stage will typically end with an output – some sort of delivery which is scheduled on a roadmap. A schedule buffer then is placed before the stage delivery milestone and protects the critical path – the sequence of tasks which defines the milestone date. Most important of course is placing the buffer **before** the delivery milestone. As the project runs, if critical path tasks lengthen the buffer can reduce, leaving the delivery date unchanged. So the buffer stabilises the delivery date.

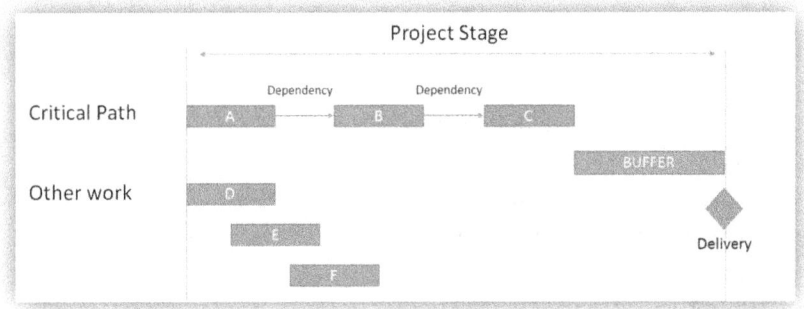

Figure 37 – Placing buffers on the critical path

Why does my buffer always get used?

There's something of a paradox around buffers and their usage. You have built your basic plan with all of your team's "most likely" estimates. And then you've added a buffer to deal with the uncertainty involved. Surely "on average" your team's estimates will be correct and so we wouldn't expect to use the buffer. How much buffer will be consumed? How often will you hit the date without using the buffer? This needs a little statistics.

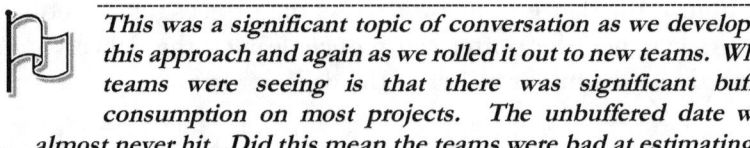 *This was a significant topic of conversation as we developed this approach and again as we rolled it out to new teams. What teams were seeing is that there was significant buffer consumption on most projects. The unbuffered date was almost never hit. Did this mean the teams were bad at estimating?*

This is an important question to the teams because they need to understand what "success" is. Is it hitting the unbuffered date or the buffered date? When we talk about task uncertainty we tend to picture a fairly accurate estimate with a small degree of uncertainty, fairly evenly spread (usually we're imagining a normal distribution). We might perhaps be saying that a task is 10 days effort +/- 1 day and we picture something as at the right.

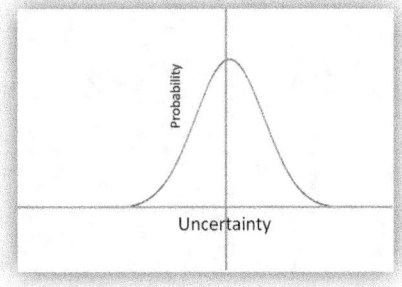

Figure 38 – Normal Distribution

This estimate splits into the "most likely" (10 days) and the uncertainty (± 1 day). Now imagine we have a sequence of N such tasks, following each other. By standard statistics, the average of the total is 10 x N days, but the fractional overrun reduces by $1/\sqrt{N}$. So if there is a 10% uncertainty for one task, there will only be a 1% uncertainty for 100 consecutive tasks. Some tasks finish early and some finish late and with more tasks this is more likely to average out. **But we know we don't see this happening!** Large projects don't tend towards the original estimates and consume less (proportional) buffer, so what are we missing?

The issue lies in the asymmetry of the uncertainty. Tasks aren't really "10 days effort ± 1 day". As discussed before, worst cases are significantly worse and best cases not very much better. Our 10 day estimate might have a best case of 9 days and a worst case of 13 days. The probability distribution will have a long "tail" and might look more like the one here. We see here that the average (mean) is now greater than the "most likely" estimate.

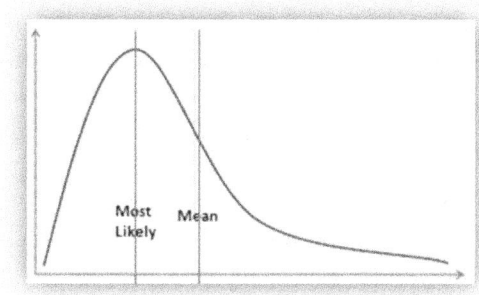

Figure 39 – Skewed Distribution

The shape of this distribution, known as a "skewed" distribution, changes everything. We built the plan based on "most likely" estimates, but the more skewed the distribution the more each task will, on average, take longer than this. This sounds strange, but for every task that overruns, several would need to underrun to compensate, because the overruns will be larger.

> As uncertainty increases buffers will be consumed even if task estimation is accurate.

In low uncertainty environments, where tasks are fairly predictable and possibly uncertainty is fairly symmetric, the effect is small. But as uncertainty increases and worst case durations increase, this inherently leads to project slip against plan.

Buffers therefore are far from a luxury. While a highly deterministic environment might not need buffering, as uncertainty levels increase, overrun becomes expected as a direct result and buffer consumption becomes expected. There is no fixed answer for "how often will we hit the unbuffered date" (except that the likelihood becomes low).

How much buffer is enough?

One key question that needs to be answered is how large are the buffers that get inserted. You can see this is going to be critical. If the buffer is too small, it fails to protect the delivery adequately. Although it will reduce the movement of the milestone, the milestone will still move. It then becomes unclear if the team has succeeded – everyone agreed on a buffered date and worked towards it, but in the end they were just "close". We want teams to be enabled to succeed, and customers to be confident in the delivery dates, so we want to avoid under buffering. But conversely we want to avoid over buffering also. If the buffers are too large, the team will be committing to dates that are too late for customers. A company that consistently over buffers will lose some competitive advantage. And if they then deliver significantly ahead of schedule in every project, the milestone dates will start to be considered "padded". Sooner or later, people will start promising earlier dates to customers and the system of "honest planning" will break down.

Quantitative Analysis

Probably the most accurate approach for sizing buffers is quantitative analysis. This is a simulation based approach based on a fully planned out project schedule, and so takes account of all constraints and dependencies. The approach is fairly simple in concept but needs some computing power to make it work – there are tools that will handle this for you.

First you build your initial project schedule with the "most likely" estimates. You also capture the "best case" and "worst case" estimates for each task. Then for each task you replace its estimate with a value somewhere between "best case" and "worst case" to represent what *might* happen. This gives you a whole new schedule, so note down where each milestone ends up. Now go back to your original schedule and generate a whole new set of task estimates between "best case" and "worst case". This gives you different milestone dates. Repeat this many times and you will generate a profile of when your milestones are likely to deliver. From this you can easily say "if you want to be 95% confident of on-time delivery, what date do you need to choose and so how much buffer is needed?"

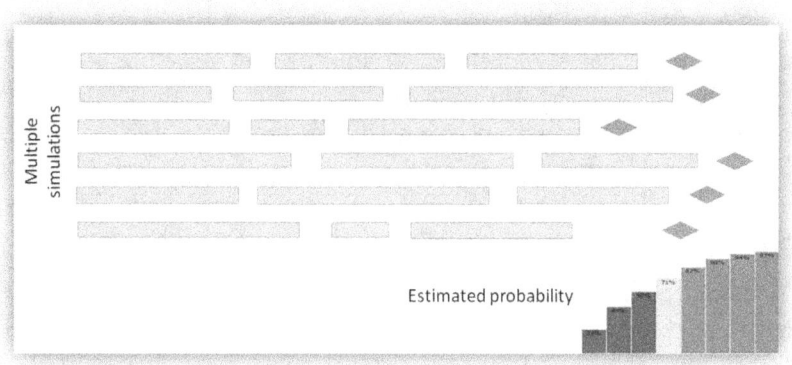

Figure 40 – Quantitative Analysis

This is a good approach in principle but relies on having specific tools. Most importantly, it needs a detailed project schedule which has all of the accurate constraints to allow the tools to recalculate the scenarios. And for most people it's a little more complex than is needed – the benefits from this level of detail are not generally required. So what can we use if we want something a little faster and easier?

We tried using Quantitative Analysis with an in-house developed tool but it proved a bit slow and over-detailed for what was needed. Our experience was that a broad understanding of level of uncertainty was enough and a fully simulated project schedule wasn't needed. Maybe schedules with more dependencies would make this a more valuable approach.

Proportional buffering

Quantitative Analysis is valuable if your project structure is complex. However a simpler approach will generally hit the Value-driven objective of getting as much value for as little overhead as possible. Proportional buffering also has the advantage that you can use it back at the task list stage and before you have any schedule, let alone a finalised one, and so avoid overcommitting early in the planning.

You have collected "most likely" and "worst case" estimates for each task. Maybe you have "best case" data as well. Now you can reserve an amount of buffer for each task. If you are familiar with PERT (Program Evaluation Review Technique, used by the U.S. Navy in the 1950s for the Polaris missile program) you will see similarities but critically we collect this into a separate buffer rather than lengthening tasks (explicit rather than implicit buffering).

How much buffer does each task add? This depends critically on how likely we are to complete the task early or late. We saw earlier that this is unlikely to be a symmetric distribution, but let's keep to a very simple model. We would normally expect to achieve somewhere between "best case" and "most likely" half the time, and somewhere between "most likely" and "worst case" half the time. Let's assume that "best case" isn't significantly better, and that if we take longer than the "most likely" estimate we have an equal chance of achieving each value between "most likely" and "worst case". That's a pretty simple model, but seems reasonable, especially since people are reluctant to finish tasks early. With this model, the average or typical time for the task is

$$\textbf{(``most likely'') + (``worst case''-``most likely'') / 4}$$

> On average we need a buffer of one quarter of the total difference between the "worst case" and "most likely" estimates.

To apply this technique, you look at all of the tasks in a section of your project (which might be a stage, perhaps subdivided to a particular team). Imagine there are 100 tasks, when we add up the "most likely" effort we have 500d of work and when we add up the "worst case" effort we have 700d of work. Now this doesn't mean that we need 200d of buffer, because not all the tasks will come out as "worst case" effort. The calculation above suggests we need a quarter of this, or 50d of buffer in this case. So we will have 500d of work in the plan and 50d of buffer. Note that this is **work**, so if we have 10 people, this will mean a 5 day schedule buffer.

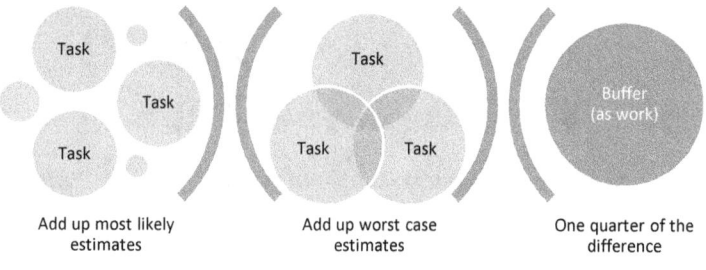

Figure 41- Sizing buffers

Chapter 9 Exercise - Project Commitment

Let us go back to the "MakeIt" project proposed in the Deterministic planning section of the book. We still have a set of design tasks totalling 200 days and a set of documentation tasks totalling 100 days. And we have a team of three designers, two authors and a lead who could do either design or documentation. We have the overheads as before of 15% leave & vacation, a management overhead of 15% and 25% of someone's time on support. But now we are going to include worst case data. The total worst case estimates for the design work are 250d and for the documentation work are 200d.

Figure 42 – "MakeIt" Project Commitment Exercise

To what schedule should you commit given this level of uncertainty? A worked answer is at the end of the book.

Chapter 10

Communicating Uncertainty

Case Study – the importance of language

The Rosetta stone

In the 18th and 19th century people marveled at the great creations of ancient Egypt. Many of the buildings would be challenging projects even today. And one feature of ancient Egyptian culture was the writing system – hieroglyphics. Here we clearly had a system of language which was present in large quantities on the ancient sites, but there seemed no chance of deciphering it because there were no modern day readers.

What happened?

The discovery of the Rosetta stone in 1799 changed the situation with hieroglyphs. The stone had the same text in three languages – hieroglyphs and two known language/writing forms (demotic and greek). Suddenly there was a reference point for hieroglyphs and by 1824 the basics of hieroglyphic writing had been decoded.

Why did this happen?

Any method of communication needs a sender and a recipient, and to be effective, the two must both understand the language being used. Before the decoding of the Rosetta stone, there were many hieroglyphs, which clearly had meaning to the senders (the ancient Egyptians), but there were no receivers able to understand the message. With the Rosetta stone setting up a mapping between the message and a known language, understanding could be built.

What can we learn?

Within a project we often forget the barriers brought by different "language". The project team must communicate in a meaningful way. Projects can be full of terms which are quite cryptic to someone outside and a way to "translate" needs to be set up. "The project has a 0.85 CPI" may as well be hieroglyphics until it is explained as "for every dollar that we spend we are achieving what we expected to cost only 85 cents". This is especially true when communicating uncertainty because there is no clearly established "language" and we are presenting hieroglyphics. We need to find a way to establish a mapping to what people want and need to understand.

What does your audience need?

Imagine you have a salesman who has arranged to meet you. A little before the meeting you get a call:

> *"Hi, it's Joe and I'm on my way to the meeting.*
> *I'm just outside town*
> *I should be at your office in a few minutes...*
> *No, hang on, I think I'll be there in ten seconds...*
> *No, sorry, it's looking more like a week."*

Traffic may be bad, but this approach will not increase your confidence in the salesman and you probably won't buy his product. But many projects report uncertainty in exactly this way. What do your customers (internal or external) want when you communicate? There are four key areas where you need to manage your communication of uncertainty.

Spatial Consistency

People want to hear the same message whomever they ask. That means that the whole team need to understand the same message around uncertainty. This can be a challenge, not least because some of the team will be having a great week and some will have spent twelve hours without sleep trying to find a really tough bug. So you need to make sure the team are involved in the story for uncertainty.

Temporal Consistency

People want to hear the same message whenever they ask. That's the issue with the salesman. No-one wants a constantly changing message as it gives nothing to use. But we know that the project will change as it runs and estimates may be modified so we need a way to introduce some stability into the messaging.

Competence

People want to be clear that the team can manage the uncertainty. Everyone knows it's there, so it's no good pretending that there isn't uncertainty. But the team have to have a message about dealing with uncertainty which gives those outside the team confidence.

Commitment

Finally your audience want to be clear how much risk is involved and who is taking it. Every business is betting on every project. The business supplies money and expects some value in return. It isn't guaranteed exactly how much money or value so there is some risk. But how much risk? And where things are not certain, is that inside the project, managed by the team, or outside, needing the stakeholders to manage the level of risk?

A language of uncertainty

Central to communicating uncertainty is the "language" of uncertainty. Most project teams talk about "when" they will deliver, but a single point in time gives no idea of the likelihood of this happening. To communicate uncertainty you need to give some idea of the spread of possible project dates. Ideally you would communicate a probability distribution that shows exactly how likely it is to achieve each possible date. However you probably don't have that level of data, and this would involve a large amount of data being associated with each delivery. Many simple approaches associate a "confidence level" with a delivery such as "this delivery is green to show it is likely to happen on time". Ideally you want to be sure that the plan date and the uncertainty data always stay together, so you want to keep the communication system simple.

The approach here is to use a pair of dates for every milestone. These dates are very clearly defined. The "plan" date is the earlier of the two dates. This represents the date that you come to by deterministic scheduling and so the date that you would use with no uncertainty. The "plan" date is a realistic and achievable date, not a "best case" figure. The "commit" date is the later date. This is the date that you are willing to commit to given the level of uncertainty in the project. The gap between the two dates is the buffer which you are holding at this milestone. To make the dates clear on reports the "plan" date is coloured red, to indicate it is high risk, while the later "commit" date is coloured green to indicate low risk.

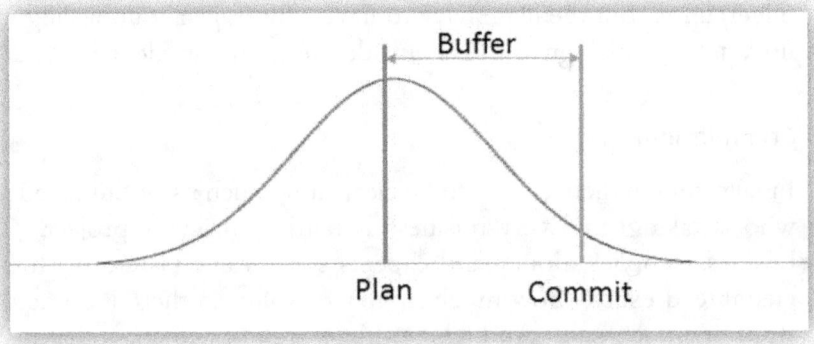

Figure 43 – Plan and Commit dates

This is a very simple way to communicate uncertainty levels, but proves very effective. Two dates, generated and managed in a standard way, are very easy to manage and to teach. Not too much data needs to be exchanged, which means that logging date pairs and ensuring they were on all of the reports was achievable. Where the "commit" date is placed will depend on how confident you need to be. Typically somewhere in the range of 80% to 95% confident might be appropriate.

Figure 44 - Date pairs

After some time of using this, teams became used to always reporting both dates for project milestones. And as the culture built up, people would start to ask for both dates – "is that red or green?" was a frequent comment if only one date is supplied. The "plan" date will move a little as the project is run and as task estimates change. But the "commit" date is a fixed point and is the one that is used with customers as a date that the team could be confident of delivering. As the approach was adopted, everyone came to value having a stable date that was realistic and achievable.

Committing in an uncertain world

Buffers are the mechanism that allows the team to make Commitments. The difference between the "Plan" and "Commit" dates is a buffer. The "Plan" date is the unbuffered date with all of the uncertainty and movement that this implies. The "Commit" date is a buffered date, with a buffer to absorb the uncertainty involved in the tasks. The buffer allows the team to make the commitment, and also stabilises the date from change. As the Plan date inevitably moves slightly over time, the Commit date is left fixed.

Surely it's not that easy?

The introduction of buffering didn't solve all of our problems with Uncertainty but it did bring in a way to discuss and manage that Uncertainty. We learned that Uncertainty management is a layer on top of deterministic planning - you can't fix a poor plan by adding buffers so your team must be good planners first. And we learned that buffers are the first areas to be questioned if people want more attractive (if less realistic) dates – you need reviewers to be asking why the plan has less buffering than other plans. But we also learned that you can plan for an early date and commit to a later one without everyone getting lazy. And even that in some cases you can tell your customer that you're doing that – they like to understand why you are confident. Mostly I think we learned that by managing Uncertainty you can allow teams a fair chance to succeed.

Chapter 11

Building better plans

Why better planning works.

Planning is only a part of project management. There are many key skills related to the execution of the project. However, good planning can be critical to the successful delivery of a project. It is easy for a team to fail before the project has started by making, or accepting, commitments to deliver something which is impossible, or would need an unlikely level of good fortune. Perhaps the team is aware that their goals are impossible, leaving them demoralised and working long hours in a vain hope to achieve them, or perhaps they continue in an optimistic haze of Groupthink until the harsh realities of late delivery.

The objective of planning is not to predict the future but to understand what you can commit to. This will avoid the project team being placed in an impossible situation. "Value-driven" planning is about focussing your limited time on the parts of planning that will help you make those commitments, maximize your chance of success and help the business get the most value as a result. We have looked at key techniques that help build value in plans, aiming to slay two of the "Four Horsemen". These techniques are intended to build effective deterministic plans and to extend into uncertain environments. I will address the final two areas in a future book.

Determinism   **Uncertainty**   **Agility**   **Risk**

Figure 45 – Two horsemen slain

There is no "magic answer" here. In some of the examples in this book we looked at the simple "MakeIt" project, summarised below.

Figure 46 – "MakeIt" Project outline

We looked at how you would estimate "MakeIt". Initially we just looked at tasks, then we brought in the overheads of running a project and then looked at uncertainty and commitment. It's worth summarising the numbers below. A simple, task-based estimate was ten weeks. By assessing a realistic project situation, this could be fourteen or fifteen weeks. And to make a commitment that we could be confident of delivering we would need to say seventeen weeks. A team that commits to the ten week figure in the planning will never be able to accommodate the difference simply by working long hours.

Tasks	Overheads	Buffer

| 0 | 2 | 4 | 6 | 8 | 10 | 12 | 14 | 16 | 18 |

Figure 47 – "MakeIt" Project timeline

This book gives a structure and approach which can be applied across many different projects. But it is not the structure or the methodology used which manages a project. A standard approach can help you build a mental picture, maybe help you communicate or avoid error. But you are the one that will be managing the project, with all its detail, its specific problems and its complex and real people.

Epilogue

At ChipCo, like at most organisations, teams worked hard, some projects went well and some went less well. And when a project went well and no-one worked late nights, the usual reaction was that the team had been lucky and had been given an easy project.

I had the good fortune to be able to peer into dark corners and look behind the scenes on many of these projects. I could see that in so many cases projects succeeded not because they were easy but because the teams did the ground work that was needed. By investing in good, robust planning the team could enable themselves to succeed in the implementation of the project.

In the early days of the company it had a crisis-driven, start-up mind-set where every project was expected to be pulled through by heroic effort. After some years, the major projects were just too important for that attitude and the culture had changed to "plan, commit, deliver". It hadn't been easy, it still wasn't perfect, but it had changed the way that planning was viewed in the organisation. And it had been a privilege to work with the teams who brought that change about.

Every man is born equal,
just some work harder in pre-season

Emmitt Smith, Dallas Cowboys, NFL

The Planning Graveyard

Through this book I have highlighted places where I have seen projects fail through insufficient planning. I have summarised these here as "The Planning Graveyard". Try and avoid your project becoming another of these tombstones.

Figure 48 – The Planning Graveyard

Value-driven Principles of Planning

I have highlighted the following which constitute key principles of Value-driven Planning. These are key places to focus your limited time and effort because they will make a difference. Deming needed 14 rules for Total Quality Management, so I feel I can manage on only 13 for Value-driven planning.

1. Project Management skills are valuable and applicable to everyone working on projects.

2. Project Management should involve at most 20% of time following methodology rules and at least 80% work specific to the project, its team and stakeholders

3. Deterministic planning skills are fundamental and all practitioners should be familiar with them.

4. The planning process must be "honest" so that the organisation and the planners genuinely wish to see teams achieve success

5. Conflict is inevitable in planning as sponsors want more for less. Conflict should be accepted at the planning stage rather than deferred to the delivery stage

6. Planning is an inclusive process. Groupthink is an enemy.

7. Scheduling activities reduces freedom for change and flexible thinking and should be done as late as possible in the planning.

8. Divide each difficulty into as many parts as is feasible and necessary to resolve it

9. Successful plans include realistic estimates for the overall project environment

10. Trust the planning work. If you've put in all of that work, don't sign up to something that you have proved is impossible

11. Dependencies should only be about hard constraints between tasks or with external inputs.

12. A plan which can be relied on has more value to the business than an unreliable plan which suggests an earlier delivery.

13. As uncertainty increases buffers will be consumed even if task estimation is accurate.

Chapter 12

Answers to Exercises

Chapter 4 Exercise - Stakeholders

You were asked to build plans to manage two stakeholders - a Sleeping Giant with a positive attitude, a high level of power over the project and a low level of interest, and a Saboteur, who has a negative attitude, high power and low interest.

For the Sleeping Giant we have a great opportunity to move this stakeholder to become a Saviour, who could be a real asset on the project. To do this we need to engage his or her enthusiasm. As with most stakeholders, the key is to understand why he or she is not interested. Most likely it's because they can't see the relevance of your project to their own goals. So you may have some selling to do. Or some communication – maybe they don't understand what the project is actually about, or they lack the technical skills to read the reports you have sent out to date.

The Saboteur is a harder problem. He or she is engaged and high power, but scores low on the attitude. This often suggests that your project is in some way a threat (perhaps you are competing for resource or promoting a competing solution). You need to understand where the issues lie and whether you can modify your project in some way to address the issues. This will mean getting the Saboteur involved. Maybe he or she could assist as a reviewer where the challenge would help avoid Groupthink. Don't ignore someone in this position – they could be a risk to success, but could even become a Saviour if you can turn them round.

Chapter 4 Exercise - Requirements

This exercise had the example Requirement below from an advertisement in 1907:

> *It should be sufficiently simple in its construction and operation to permit an intelligent man to become proficient in its use within a reasonable length of time*

Clearly the statements here are very subjective. How simple is "sufficiently simple"? How intelligent is "intelligent"? How proficient is "proficient"? What is a "reasonable" length of time?

These do not seem to be verifiable, and subjective measures rarely lead to agreed success. Such a vague Requirement would lead to problems later in the project. Imagine you gave this Requirement to a contractor – you would have to pay almost regardless of what they gave you in return.

To be fair to the US Army, they clearly appreciated the issues and this is just an introduction in the original advertisement. The advertisement went on to include some much less generic and much more appropriate Requirements such as the one below. This is a far better project Requirement as it is clearly stated, verifiable and even specifies how it will be verified. The team could be confident of knowing if they had achieved success here.

> *Should be designed to have a speed of at least forty miles per hour in still air.*
> *The speed will be determined by taking an average of the time over a measured course of more than five miles against and with the wind.*

Chapter 5 Exercise – Product Breakdown

For this exercise, you needed to make a PBS (Product Breakdown Structure) for the parts for a bicycle.

You could, for example, break the bicycle down by functional units into, say, wheels, gears, frame, seat and brakes. And then sub-divide these to generate the individual elements as below. This is one possible solution and you may have something similar – don't worry too much about the details and language unless you're a bike expert.

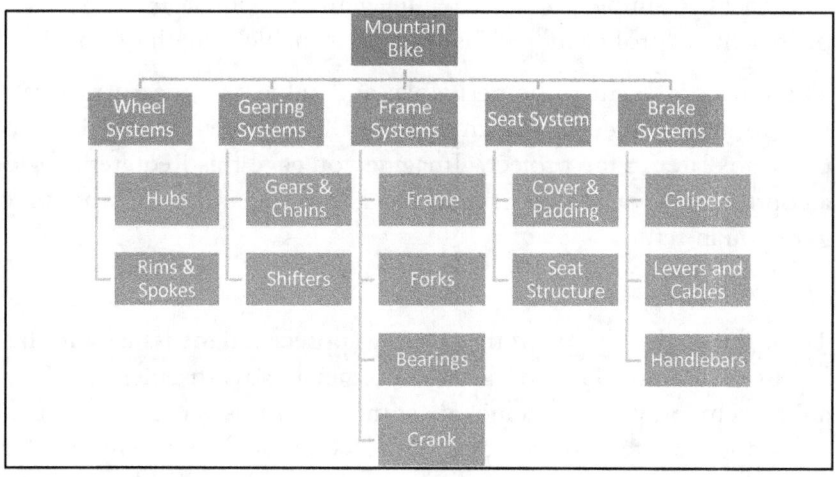

Figure 49 – Product Breakdown Exercise (1)

But there is something unsatisfactory with this as a solution. It makes a lot of assumptions about the design and is clearly drawn by someone who already has seen a bicycle. In many ways that is "cheating" for a plan. What if you don't already know the answer? So to address this we have the alternative PBS below. As you see, the same 13 end outputs have been identified, but the approach of breaking it down is different. Instead of focussing on the structure of the end product, this PBS is built around the functional needs of the user. This is a more generic way to evolve a PBS, because you are truly breaking down the requirement without already having designed a solution

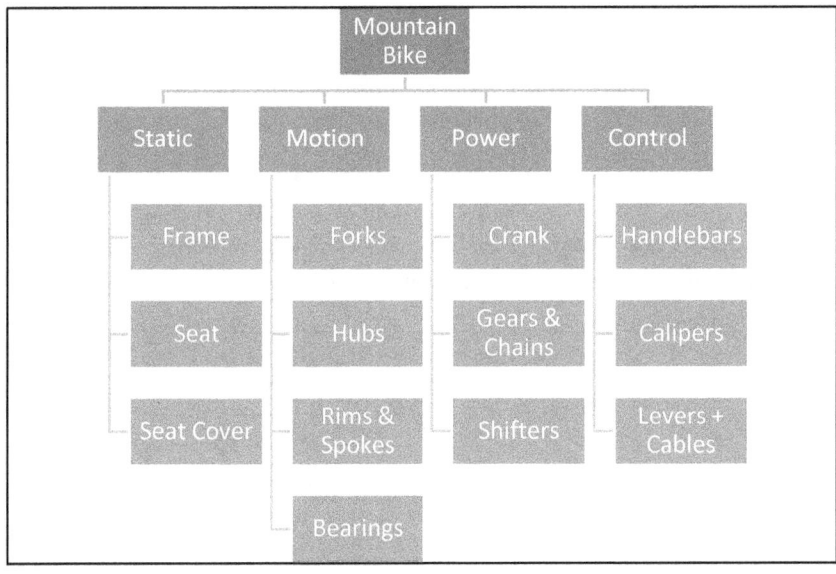

Figure 50 – Product Breakdown Exercise (2)

Chapter 6 Exercise – "MakeIt" Project Sizing

Figure 51 – "MakeIt" Project Sizing Exercise

We're planning for a stage of a project in which we have a set of design tasks totalling 200 days and a set of documentation tasks totalling 100 days. These are independent (so we don't have to wait for any task to complete). And we have a team of three designers, two authors and a lead who could do either design or documentation

If we put the lead with the designers then we have 4 designers to do 200d of work, which is 50 days of elapsed time. And we have two authors to do 100d work, which is again 50 days of elapsed time. We are assuming these are independent so the whole stage will finish in 50 elapsed days.

Chapter 6 Exercise – "MakeIt" Product Overhead

Figure 52 – "MakeIt" Project Overheads Exercise

With overhead, our calculations are a bit more complicated. We still have a set of design tasks totalling 200 days and a set of documentation tasks totalling 100 days. And we have a team of three designers, two authors and a lead who could do either design or documentation. But now we have 15% vacation & training, a management overhead of 15% and 25% of someone's time on support.

We have a team of 5 to manage (excluding the lead who will be managing). Looking at the management overhead, 5x15%=75% so we will be losing 75% of the lead to manage the others. Let's put the remaining 25% of the lead's time on helping the designers which gives us 3.25 designers. And we'll take the 25% support requirement and assign this to an author. So now we have 3.25 designers to do 200 days of work, but with 15% leave, and 1.75 authors to do 100 days of work, again with 15% leave: We include the leave by dividing the time by 0.85.

- Design work: 200 / 3.25 / 0.85 = 72 days elapsed
- Documentation: 100 / 1.75 / 0.85 = 67 days elapsed

So the project will take about 14-15 weeks to deliver with realistic levels of overheads.

Chapter 7 Exercise - Scheduling

In this exercise you are building a schedule based on a given task list. You should start the exercise by looking at the constraints. There is a Gantt chart below with three sections for function A, function B and the integration work. The named bars represent the tasks. Cindy's name is against the two tasks which require her. Otherwise there are no assignments yet. The size of the tasks on the schedule assumes one full time person assigned to each. The dependencies are shown by arrowed lines, and I have started to schedule the tasks based on these dependencies. Now what about the Critical Path? This goes through **Coding A -> Testing A -> User Testing -> Release packaging** and we can see that lengthening any of these will push out the end date. I've marked it with a dotted line below.

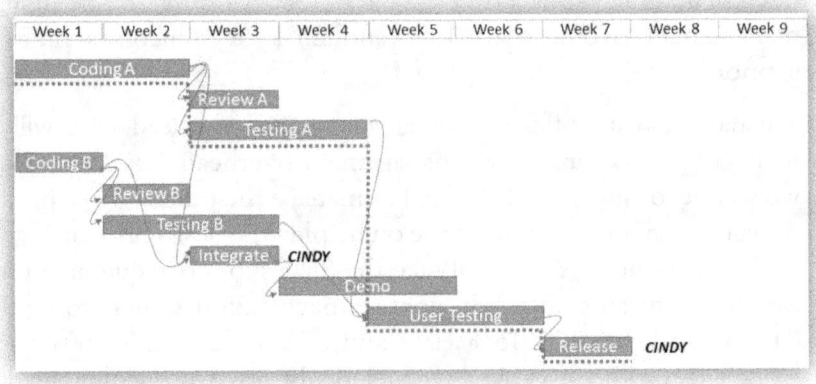

Figure 53 – Scheduling Exercise (1)

But this isn't our final schedule yet. Next we need to make the task assignments. How will we do this? Individuals are not interchangeable here. Cindy already has some assignments. Most critically, Bill is only available 50% of the time. This means that if I assign Bill to a task, it will take twice as long as shown. There's a slight trap here. The "Coding A" task is less *effort* with Bill on it, but with only 50% availability it is still more *time*. Now remember we have identified our Critical Path. If I assign Bill on the Critical Path, the tasks will lengthen and the project will deliver later. So that then drives my solution. I can use Alex for the Critical path activities, and then fill in the gaps as below.

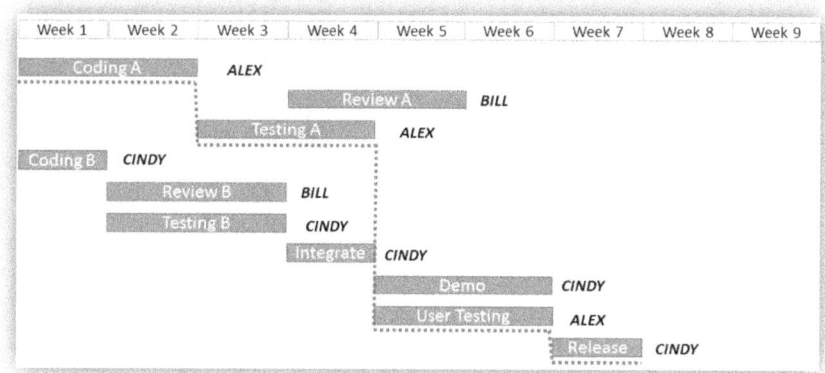

Figure 54 – Scheduling Exercise (2)

So what do we see in the schedule after the assignments (and after we have levelled to make sure no-one is over-loaded)? We've protected the Critical Path and so the overall project length is unchanged. Alex and Cindy are kept busy through the project. I've put Bill on the review tasks, which have lengthened as a result. There's some potential risk that review feedback may come in late from this, although I hadn't formally declared this was a dependency in the exercise. I'm quite pleased about keeping Bill off the Critical Path – he's a nice guy but I only have 50% of his time and such estimates are notoriously unreliable. If there's a crisis elsewhere he may suddenly be unavailable for my project, so it's best to keep the flexibility.

Chapter 9 Exercise - Project Commitment

Figure 55 – "MakeIt" Project Commitment Exercise

We still have a set of design tasks totalling 200 days and a set of documentation tasks totalling 100 days. And we have a team of three designers, two authors and a lead who could do either design or documentation. And we have 15% vacation & training, a management overhead of 15% and 25% of someone's time on support.

But now we are going to include worst case data. The total worst case estimates for the design work are 250d and for the documentation work are 200d. In the previous exercise, we had assigned 3.25 people to the design work and 1.75 to the documentation. We use the proposed formula of one quarter of the increase in estimates as a buffer. This gives the schedule below:

- Design work: $(200 + 50/4) / 3.25 / 0.85 = 77$ days elapsed
- Documentation: $(100 + 100/4) / 1.75 / 0.85 = 84$ days elapsed

So a schedule that we can commit to with these levels of uncertainty would be around 17 weeks. Note that with the most likely estimates, the Design work was the longest part of the project, but taking the uncertainty into account, we now find the documentation is likely to be the "long pole".

It is worth just thinking about the three numbers generated in the "MakeIt" exercises. Just adding up the task list gave us an estimate of 10 weeks. By adding in the overheads of running a realistic project, this increases to 14 weeks. And if you expect to make a commitment to deliver, this would be based on delivery in 17 weeks.

www.ingramcontent.com/pod-product-compliance
Lightning Source LLC
Chambersburg PA
CBHW070300190526
45169CB00001B/486